Praise for
The One

"Ryan and Amanda have a truly amazing—and viral—love story. We've not only read the book, we know this couple personally, and they are the real deal. *The One* tells their fascinating story, but it's also chock-full of invaluable tips and practical approaches for anyone looking for lifelong love."

—Drs. Les and Leslie Parrott, authors
of *Saving Your Marriage Before It Starts*

"Ryan and Amanda Leak's story is both inspiring and insightful. It's spontaneous romance coupled with historic wisdom from Scripture, making their story enticing to over one million people on YouTube. In *The One,* you'll discover the ingredients to their story that will also help make your story a success!"

—Ron Luce, president/CEO of Teen
Mania International

"Upon meeting the Leaks, you can't help but see how they both reflect Jesus. From how they met to how they live now, it's amazing to see the way they use their gifts and talents as communicators to reinforce what love is: it's a surprise and a commitment. Both Amanda and Ryan are continuously sharing this message in all that they do."

—Bianca Juarez Olthoff, speaker and chief
storyteller at The A21 Campaign

"In an era when love needs clarity and traditional marriage seems naive, Ryan and Amanda present a practical, entertaining (romantic) apologetic, which appeals to the deep intuitions and longings of the human heart. This love story guides attitudes and behaviors into the fabulous opportunity biblical marriage was designed to provide. Whether beginning your personal love story or continuing to accelerate established love, this book will return your investment."

—PASTOR JIM HENNESY, senior pastor at Trinity
Church and author of *No More Cotton Candy*

THE ONE

THE ONE

An Amazing Love Story Starts with You

RYAN & AMANDA LEAK

WITH JODI LIPPER

WATERBROOK
PRESS

THE ONE
PUBLISHED BY WATERBROOK PRESS
12265 Oracle Boulevard, Suite 200
Colorado Springs, Colorado 80921

Details in some anecdotes and stories have been changed to protect the identities of the persons involved.

Hardcover ISBN 978-1-60142-744-1
eBook ISBN 978-1-60142-746-5

Cover design by Kristopher K. Orr; cover photo by Meshail Mitchell

Published in the United States by WaterBrook Multnomah, an imprint of the Crown Publishing Group, a division of Penguin Random House LLC, New York.

WATERBROOK and its deer colophon are registered trademarks of Penguin Random House LLC.

Library of Congress Cataloging-in-Publication Data
Leak, Ryan.
    The one : an amazing love story starts with you / by Ryan and Amanda Leak ; with Jodi Lipper.—First Edition.
        pages cm
    ISBN 978-1-60142-744-1 (hardback)—ISBN 978-1-60142-746-5 (electronic) 1. Marriage—Religious aspects—Christianity. 2. Leak, Ryan. 3. Leak, Amanda. I. Leak, Amanda. II. Lipper, Jodi. III. Title.
    BV835.L425 2015
    248.8'44—dc23

                                                    2015004312

Printed in the United States of America
2015—First Edition

10 9 8 7 6 5 4 3 2 1

SPECIAL SALES
Most WaterBrook Multnomah books are available at special quantity discounts when purchased in bulk by corporations, organizations, and special-interest groups. Custom imprinting or excerpting can also be done to fit special needs. For information, please e-mail SpecialMarkets @WaterBrookMultnomah.com or call 1-800-603-7051.

To the little boy who keeps us grounded and makes us better people every day, we dedicate this book to you, Jaxson Carter Leak.

Contents

Foreword

When I was a twenty-six-year-old graduate student, I became very close friends with a wonderful man named Jeff. He was a few years older, the leader of a student Christian fellowship group, and we shared some similar activities. (Truth be told, I just *might* have joined one of the activities because of him . . .) We were just friends, but we spent lots of time together, and I wondered, *Might it become something more?*

Shortly before he graduated, Jeff asked me out for lunch and told me that he'd been praying about the same thing. He said he wanted to stay away from anything romantic for a while and really dive into a much more purposeful friendship to see if we might be "the one" for each other. We began talking about everything: our histories, goals, dreams, worries, and weaknesses. We counseled with friends and mentors. I was advised to not just pray, "Lord, is he the one?" but, "Lord, if this is of You, make *me* the one: make me into the woman Jeff needs as a wife. And make him into the man I need as a husband."

Twenty years later, I look back with awe at how God has answered those prayers. How He honored that effort to not only find the right person, but to *be* the right person. How he guided two normal, semiselfish, excited-but-clueless people into a true love story. And how He ensured that we found each other in the first place.

As I watch the amazing story of Ryan and Amanda Leak on their famous YouTube video and read about their transition from friendship to marriage, I see an echo of my own history. But as I absorb the vibrant wisdom God has given them to share, I see so many of the lessons I wish I had known during our excited-but-clueless phase!

In this engaging book, Ryan and Amanda as a newlywed millennial couple bring to bear insight far beyond their years. They share solid counsel and encouragement for everyone who has wondered if the right person is around the corner—and real, practical advice for not only finding "the one" but *being* that one who someone else is looking for . . . both now and for years to come.

I'm thrilled that a few years ago, a simple little engaged-and-married-in-the-same-day video went viral and has given this remarkable couple a chance to share a big message today. A message that all of us need to hear.

Shaunti Feldhahn

Best-selling author of *For Women Only*

Introduction

What makes an amazing love story? Is it witty conversation over dinner, common interests, shared values, and strength in the face of obstacles, or is it something else—some secret, elusive element that we can only pray for? We've all seen those couples, the ones holding hands in the park or whispering to each other as they stare into one another's eyes, as if they share an awesome secret. We watch them and wonder, *What's the big secret?* And more importantly, what's their story? Do they ever argue? What makes them tick? How did their relationship start, and how did they end up with such an amazing love story?

We never anticipated becoming one of those couples. When we met, we simply tried to listen to God and find out what kind of journey He wanted to take us on. And while we faced a lot of obstacles along the way, it turns out that the story He had planned for us was one that many other people were interested in, and one that we couldn't wait to share with the rest of the world.

Three months into our new marriage, we posted a video about our surprise wedding on YouTube. The previous three months had been the happiest we'd ever known and not nearly as hard as people told us they would be. After a weeklong honeymoon, we'd moved in together, picked out a bunch of shows on Netflix, and hardly left the apartment for a couple of weeks. We're so grateful that our jobs as motivational speakers and young-adult directors at our church allowed us this time to get to know each other as husband and wife.

The night we posted our video, we were sitting on the couch watching a show when we saw that one of our friends had tweeted that our video had gotten ten thousand views. We couldn't believe it. Did we even know ten thousand people? We ignored the show as we tried to name every person we knew, but we fell asleep before we even got through the first thousand.

In the months that followed, the number of views of our video skyrocketed past a hundred thousand, then five hundred thousand, and finally over one million. As those numbers climbed, our lives and our marriage took a brand-new path, one that we never imagined for ourselves. We appeared on national television, were interviewed for global newspapers, and even had a chance to meet some of our favorite celebrities. We slowly realized along the way that things were going to look different for us. We were in no way excused from the challenging realities of marriage, but we were following a unique and unknown path. God had written our love story, and He wanted to share it with the world.

We quickly started receiving thousands of e-mails, messages, and tweets from young adults telling us how our story inspired them, made them rethink everything they believed about love, and even led them closer to Christ. Along with these heartfelt responses, questions about dating and relationships inevitably poured in. As we embraced this season of our lives, we had the opportunity to meet and speak with thousands of young adults all over the country. We met girls who'd grown up without fathers or any male role models and now struggled to trust any male in their lives. We met guys who believed they were supposed to lead their relationships spiritually and financially but actually had no idea what this even meant. We heard from girls who'd been hurt in the past and were struggling to keep their faith that love even existed in this world and from guys who thought they didn't deserve love because they were broke. Hearing all their stories reinforced something that we already knew—relationships are complicated and hard—and now we saw it from a whole new perspective.

More than anything, we saw that so many of these young adults were in love with the idea of love. They were so busy waiting for someone amazing to show up, instead of spending this time becoming an amazing person themselves. One girl we met, Erica, had followed a guy across the country, hoping to marry him in the near future. Ten years later, after he had fathered two children with other women while still living with Erica, she finally had the courage to move on with her life and ask him to move out. When we heard this story, we desperately wished we could have gone back ten years, taken her aside, heard her heart, and encouraged her to make better decisions.

What we can do instead is encourage you to make good choices starting now. No matter what sort of relationships you've had in the past, we want you to know that God has a destiny, a plan, and a strategy for your life and relationships, and the great news is that with His help you can start writing a new story for your life today. Erica can't go back ten years and change anything, but she can decide to do something different with her *next* ten years. And so can you.

People who watched our wedding documentary believed our love story was all about getting engaged, getting married, and saying "I love you" for the first time, all on the same day. That was part of it. But before that day, we went through a five-year journey together, through ups and downs, challenges, obstacles, joy, and persistence. During those five years, we took steps to create a great relationship, but we also made plenty of mistakes. When we saw those same mistakes being repeated by the young adults we spoke to every day as the young-adult directors of our church, we knew that we had to find a way to share with them the advice we wished someone had given us five years before.

The path to marriage includes those complicated dating years when the rules aren't always clear and certainly aren't fair. So much of your success when it comes to relationships is based on the way you were raised. If your parents modeled a healthy relationship for you, then you've got a head start toward creating a healthy marriage for yourself. If your parents showed you something less healthy or weren't around to model any sort of relationship, you may feel like just imagining your future is an uphill battle. You have a few options to pull guidance from, but there's no earthly model for a perfect marriage.

The church is a good place to start, but it can feel that the majority of sermons are geared toward married couples with kids. During the few times a year when churches touch on dating and relationships, often around Valentine's Day, most of their advice is a list of things you *shouldn't* be doing instead of the things you could and should be doing to become the best you. While we agree with most of this advice in theory, we know it doesn't always answer all your questions.

Another option is to take your clues from the media. While there are some great resources out there that are really helping people, most people don't know where to find them and subconsciously believe that falling in love should be their goal because that's what our society cele-brates most. Instead of showing you how to create a healthy relation-ship, our culture simply gives you an image to aspire to, one that will make you appear to be more dateable. Most of what the media presents about love is completely false, and taking too many of your clues from "reality" shows that have nothing to do with the reality of marriage can actually cause a lot of damage to your relationships.

If you fall for this trap, you'll start to believe that if you drive the right car, wear the right clothes, say the right things, and have a sweet house or loft, then you're a keeper. Well, we don't even know you, but we can say without a doubt that you're better than that. If you're look-ing for an average relationship, that's fine. You can put down this book. No hard feelings. But if you're looking for something better than aver-age—an amazing love story and a godly relationship—then you've come to the right place.

Today, we are so grateful for the challenges we faced when we were dating because they're exactly what forced us to seek wisdom from mar-ried couples, pastors, and trusted mentors and friends. We went to coun-seling separately and together to heal from past hurts and become fully whole before joining together to become one. As a result, we set up healthy habits in our dating life that allowed us to transition easily into marriage. We aren't perfect—far from it. We've stumbled a bit along the way, and we're happy to share our failures along with our successes.

We're inviting you to read about our triumphs and our mistakes, and along the way we'll offer practical guidance, encouragement, re-minders, questions to ask yourself, and helpful practices you can begin today. No matter what your relationship status may be, these will set the foundation for a healthy, thriving marriage in the future. We absolutely believe in "the one," and we believe that you're it. You're the one who can make the decision either to follow the path to an average future or to use this time to prepare yourself for something more—your destiny. God has something awesome in mind for you, but He can't get you there without your help. Make up your mind to reject average and to start living up to your potential in love and in life. An amazing love story starts with you.

1

Engaged and Married in One Day

Father, we thank you today that in your Word, you set it up so that people actually do come together where two do become one. And then when You're there, the third strand in that wound-up thing that You're putting together holds it tightly. We sense Your presence in this place. We sense You here, but we also know that as these two have chosen to follow You, they cannot do it without You.

—Nate Ruch, pastor at our wedding

SHE'S THE ONE

Ryan

Before I met Amanda, I never would have said that I was looking for a girl I could bring home to meet my mother. I'm not a mama's boy, but at the same time I knew my mother could be a little picky, especially when it came to me, the youngest of her three sons. In the past I'd flirted with some girls and dated a little, but I never considered bringing any of those girls home to meet my mother. I never even talked to my mom about the girls I dated, but when I first saw Amanda Roman walk into my brother's church, one of the first thoughts that popped into my head was, *I bet Mom would love her.*

Until that moment, I thought I had years to travel the world, do my business, and go to Lakers games before settling down. I was content and busy in my life as a "pastor-preneur," running two businesses: a motion-graphics company and a staffing company. I also traveled the country as an itinerant speaker and consultant. Life was busy and good. I was in no rush to get married.

But God had other plans. My brother was a worship pastor in Atlanta, and Amanda was in a discipleship program at his church. He called me and said, "I found your wife." I laughed him off. "Yeah, I'll bet you did," I said, but when I went to visit him a few weeks later and Amanda walked into the room, everything changed.

Amanda changed what I was looking for and defined my "type." She had an aura about her that commanded a room, just the right amount of spice, and the world's most captivating smile. I had no way of knowing then if she was the one, but I definitely hoped she was. And

I knew that if she didn't turn out to be the one for me, whoever did would now have a lot to live up to. Amanda set a new standard for me.

Nearly four years later, after our relationship was tested in a million different ways and we'd each grown fully ready for marriage, Amanda and her friend were hanging out at my apartment while I was making dinner. I was going in and out of the room as they moved from one topic to another, finally landing on girl talk about weddings. It was a casual conversation; I'm not sure Amanda even knew I could hear her when she remarked offhandedly to her friend that she wanted to get engaged and married on the same day.

I didn't say a word, but I was thinking, *What? What does that even mean? How could it possibly work?* As I stood in the kitchen, it slowly dawned on me that in order to get engaged and married on the same day and still have the type of wedding Amanda dreamed of (not just a town-hall wedding), I would have to plan the entire wedding in secret. We've all heard of surprise birthday parties and even surprise engagement parties, but who's ever heard of a surprise wedding?

At that point, Amanda and I had been through a lot together, and I knew beyond a shadow of a doubt that she was the woman I wanted to marry. It was just a question of when, and I knew that if I was going to be planning the entire wedding by myself, I'd better get started right away. First I needed to learn more about weddings in general. I immediately thought of Paula, a classy woman from my church who's like a second mother to me.

A few days later, I went to the church and grabbed Candis, a young woman who I knew could give me the perspective of a female from my own generation and pulled her into Paula's office. I closed the door and said, "I want you to remain calm, but I have to tell you something." A huge smile immediately broke out on each of their faces. "You're going to propose!" Paula exclaimed. Candis jumped up to hug me. "I wish it was that simple," I told them. As she sat back down, I explained. "Amanda said it was her dream to get engaged and married on the same day."

Candis looked at me, pure confusion on her face. "What?" she asked, as if she hadn't heard me. Paula's reaction was a little different. She'd understood what I'd said, but she was frowning. "Ryan," she said gently, with a mother's worry, "I don't know if that's such a good idea." Their reactions told me exactly how crazy this idea sounded.

"I need to know what goes into planning a wedding," I told them, "and what it's going to cost." I grabbed a napkin and started taking notes as they gave me a crash course in wedding planning, from the dress and the tux to the flowers, catering, music, photographer, and even the cake.

Once I knew the basics of wedding planning, I needed to find out exactly what Amanda wanted her wedding to be like. Luckily, a lot of our friends were getting married, so we had plenty of opportunities to talk about weddings in general. After every wedding and even in the middle of dates, I asked Amanda what she thought about certain details and what she'd do differently. After dropping her off at home, I furiously made notes in my phone so I wouldn't forget what she'd said.

Whenever the topic of weddings came up, I tried to keep it super casual so I wouldn't give anything away. I wanted it to seem like I was thinking about it every now and then instead of during every waking moment of my life. Finally I called her at work one day and said, "Let's be honest about our families' situations. If and when we get married, the cost of the wedding is going to be on us, so I want to start saving for it now." Amanda paused, and I wondered if she thought it was odd that I was bringing this up when we weren't even engaged yet. But we both knew that marriage was in our future. "That's a good idea," Amanda said finally. "Great, I'll handle the numbers," I told her, "and you write down everything you'd want at your dream wedding. I'll price everything out and set a budget."

I figured it would take Amanda a few days or weeks to write down all the details of her dream wedding, but the girl e-mailed me an extremely thorough document within an hour. Now I knew who she wanted to sing at her wedding, who she wanted in the wedding party, what sort of venue she wanted, and all sorts of other minute details. I had my work cut out for me.

Once I priced everything out, I set a budget for the entire event and took a hard look at my own finances. I needed to know how much I could set aside each month and how much extra work I needed to take on in the next six months in order to pay for all of it. I quickly realized that even if I really hustled, it was going to be extremely tight. Luckily, I had Amanda as my partner, and she's a great saver. I crunched a few more numbers and then e-mailed her back and asked her to start setting aside a certain amount each month. Amanda may not have known what I was planning, but we were already in it together.

Getting married in Miami wasn't on Amanda's wish list, but a friend of mine who lived down there convinced me that it would be the perfect location for our wedding. When I told Amanda a few days later that I was flying to Miami for "work," she immediately said, "Ugh, I hate Miami." Uh-oh. But when I saw how beautiful the beach was down there and found a hotel that was exactly what we were looking for and fit our budget, I knew my friend was right. I told myself it was an added bonus that Amanda hated Miami because she would never expect it to be the place we got married or even engaged. It would be a real surprise.

The next several months seemed like a giant test of my will. Keeping this enormous secret from the person I loved most while making sure no one else spilled the beans had me constantly on edge. Until a couple of months before the wedding, nobody except my brothers and a very small handful of friends knew what I was planning. I didn't want to risk Amanda finding out. Most people didn't find out until they were invited, and even then I kept the details from specific people I didn't trust with the secret.

I woke up every morning asking myself, *Is today the day that I'm going to fail?* While I was at the gym, shooting hoops, or even speaking to large crowds, in the back of my mind I was running through the guest list, wondering who might slip and what I could do to stop them. But as each day passed and the secret remained intact, I got closer to making the surprise wedding a reality.

It was hard not to focus solely on the wedding, but I knew it was even more important for us to prepare for marriage since our engagement period would be hours instead of months or years. A few months before the wedding, I told Amanda that I wanted to attend a premarital class that was for couples who were engaged, seriously dating, or simply thinking about marriage. It was a great class that helped us get to know each other on an even deeper level. The talking points we received served as jumping-off points for imagining and discussing our future relationship, home, and even children. I already knew that I wanted to marry Amanda, but after completing that class, I felt more confident than ever that we could work together to build a healthy, thriving, godly marriage.

A Dream Day

Amanda

When Ryan and I were dating, it seemed like every other day another one of our friends was getting engaged. One by one, I watched them start planning the day they'd spent their entire lives dreaming about and get incredibly stressed out—and rightfully so! I was in school full time and working a full-time job, and I couldn't imagine planning a wedding on top of everything else that was already on my plate. I like to say I'm a simple girl who knows what she likes and wants what she wants, and I knew that my laser-focused personality plus work, school, and planning a dream wedding would add up to self-destruction.

My friend, who's also named Amanda, is an event coordinator who plans a lot of weddings. She was hanging out with Ryan and me one night sharing stories about some of the stressed-out brides she'd worked with. "Everyone thinks it's glamorous," she told me, "but they don't know that half the time you're starving, hiding in the back trying to eat a pretzel for strength while a bride's yelling at you because she's so stressed out!" I'm usually a relaxed person, but suddenly I could picture myself on my wedding day running around in a white dress on a caffeine high, panicking because the florist sent roses instead of peonies. "And now everyone wants a theme wedding," Amanda continued. "Every wedding has to be completely unique. It's so much pressure."

I thought about this for a moment and then said, "You know what would be really different? I'd love to get engaged in the morning and married that same night." I'd never thought of this before. It just popped into my head as we were talking. Amanda looked at me as if I was crazy and asked, "But how would you plan a wedding the day of?" I just shrugged this off. I was already caught up in the fantasy of one day filled with two celebrations: the engagement and the wedding.

With no time to stress about anything, we'd be forced to go with the flow and remember what's really important. I could imagine my loud Puerto Rican family getting really excited about the whole thing and spending the day laughing and having fun. After the engagement, I'd run to the store with my closest friends and the godsisters who I grew up with and are like my best friends and sisters combined. Together, we'd pick out a cute dress for each of them right off the rack. We'd play whatever music happened to be on our iPods.

It would all be spontaneous and fun with no rules, stress, or pressure to be perfect, almost like eloping but better because our families would be there. Amanda and I joked and fantasized about this for a while, but I didn't give it much more thought after that because I figured that logistically it would be impossible. And without Ryan, it would have been.

With all the work I had to get through my senior year, I enjoyed taking a break from the grind by fantasizing about our wedding—what it would look like, who would be there, and what Ryan and I would each be thinking and feeling the whole time. Meanwhile, I had no idea that Ryan was secretly planning the whole thing without me! For months, my friends had been egging me on every time I talked about a potential wedding. At first I thought *I* was weird for thinking about a wedding before an engagement, but they made me feel like it was the most normal thing ever. Since everyone I knew was in on the surprise, they encouraged the dreaming.

Eventually they urged me to start looking for a dress. I brushed this off until one day my friend Des and I wandered past a wedding-dress boutique. Before we went in I told her, "I am NOT buying anything. Just looking around." I tried on two or three dresses just for fun. Then on my way back to the fitting room, I saw a gorgeous mermaid-style dress with lace details and a tulle bottom. Des saw the way I was looking at that dress and said, "Try it on!"

As soon as I put the dress on, I knew it was the one. After spending twenty minutes in the dressing room with Des telling her that I couldn't be the girl who had a dress before a ring, the sales lady came back and told me that she could get me the dress for $300 under my budget. I was still torn, so I called Ryan and explained the situation, worried that he was going to think I was crazy. To my surprise, he said it was a great idea and that I should go for it. This should have probably been a huge giveaway, but I had no idea. I never stopped and thought, *Hmm . . . I wonder if my boyfriend is planning a surprise wedding for me.* My one and only suspicion was that my friends knew a proposal was in the works.

A Perfect Storm

Ryan

The day before the wedding, we had one hundred guests flying in on about seventy-five different flights, and out of those, only one flight was cancelled—Amanda's. At about 4 p.m. the day before the wedding, she called me from the airport and said, "Hey, my flight's cancelled." She had zero urgency because she had no idea that she was getting married the next day. She thought she was flying to Miami to help some friends of ours move and probably thought she'd lucked out! But I just about lost my mind. Amanda was walking around the Dallas airport drinking Starbucks like it was nothing, while I was pacing the hotel lobby, zeroing in on how I was going to get Amanda to Miami. Deep down, I knew that God would make it happen if it was meant to work out, but it was still pretty stressful.

I spent hours researching alternate flights, and Amanda finally got on a flight that landed in Miami around midnight. I was so relieved to have her there that I was just about shaking when I picked her up from the airport. But the next morning, the sun was shining, all was well, and I was excited about getting married. The first thing I thought about when I woke up in my hotel room was the fact that I am extremely blessed. I think you can tell how blessed a person is by the relationships he has, and the fact that one hundred people had flown to Miami and would be in the hotel lobby to support me and Amanda was humbling and inspiring. I knew that with them on our side, we couldn't fail.

I picked Amanda up at her hotel room with Jeff, the videographer I'd hired to film the entire thing. I'd told Amanda that we were making a video for the youth group that our friend who was moving to Miami was running, but that didn't really explain why he was filming us just hanging out. She looked beautiful and happy, but she was being quiet in front of the camera. Amanda knew me well enough by then to know what a dreamer I am and to be prepared to go with the flow when we're together. I'd planned plenty of crazy dates and adventures over the past five years, and some of them worked out great while others were total flops.

Of course, there were plenty that fell in between, too. For one Valentine's Day I bought Amanda a nice dress and some new jewelry and made reservations at a fancy restaurant. We were all set to go when my car broke down. We had to take Amanda's car, which we called Jagger because it was so old and broken down, with the front bumper hanging off. And it had moves like Jagger. That car had the shakes. We pulled up to the four-star restaurant and asked the valet guys to take a picture of us all dressed up next to our piece-of-junk car. One of the things I most love about Amanda is her willingness to go along with my schemes.

I think Amanda knew I was up to something the morning of the engagement/wedding, but thankfully she went along with it then, too. We were walking down the hallway with the camera guy following us when two ladies who worked at the hotel stopped us and asked, "Are you famous?" I told them I wasn't famous, so they asked, "Then why is there a camera following you?" I calmly said, "I'm actually in the middle of proposing." That's literally how Amanda found out what was going on, just moments before I proposed.

As much as I like having a grand plan, I never wanted things to feel so scripted that they didn't seem real. Over the past several months, I'd been so busy and stressed planning everything to the letter, and now I just wanted to be done planning and let the moment unfold naturally. I was ready to be as raw and real as possible, focused on how good it felt to be with Amanda and to not have anything to hide.

One thing that's kind of unique about our relationship is that until the moment I proposed, I never told Amanda that I loved her. I'd found plenty of other ways to show my affection, but those words meant so much to me that I didn't want to say them until I knew I could back them up with every fiber of my being. By that day, Amanda and I had been through so much, and I knew I'd proven how I felt so I could believe myself when I said the words. I'd been practicing this moment in the shower for months, but I still wasn't prepared. There was no script here. I got down on one knee in the beautiful outdoor area in front of the hotel and said, "Amanda Roman, I love you so much, and it would honor me if you would marry me."

As soon as those words were out of my mouth, all of the stress and worry about planning the wedding fell away. Amanda nodded a yes with tears in her eyes and a shocked smile all over her face, and I slid the ring onto her finger. As we kissed, I could not believe that this was really happening. There was a part of me that still thought something would go wrong.

A MOMENT OF REFLECTION

Amanda

I was at the airport with my friend Shirley, who was moving to Miami, when we found out that our flight was cancelled. A few hours later, Ryan got me on another flight alone. I felt so bad leaving Shirley behind, and it didn't seem to make any sense for me to get there before the person who was actually moving. I told her I'd just wait with her, but she insisted that I go. In the back of my mind, I thought, *Wow, she re-*

ally wants me to get to Miami. What is she up to? I wondered if it was because Ryan was going to propose in Miami, so I jumped on the plane without asking any more questions. "See you in Miami, Shirley!"

It ended up being perfect for me to fly there alone because it gave me much-needed time for reflection. Writing in my journal, I told God that as I was growing up I'd seen Him provide for me through my mom. As a single mom, money was tight, but something always came through when we needed it. My grandparents would help us out, or my mom would find out about an organization that was giving out food or helping with rent. Other times we'd have just enough gas to get to my godparents' house where there was plenty of food and love to go around. But over the past few years, I'd really seen God provide for me personally. Thinking about this made me feel overwhelmed with love and gratitude. On that flight to Miami, I told God that I knew it wasn't His plan for me to grow up without a dad, but considering that's what had happened, He'd provided more than enough for me and even given me some sweet surprises along the way. I finished by thanking him for the blessing of Ryan and wrote, "I'm ready for this next chapter, whatever it is. So surprise me."

I barely slept that night; I was just too excited, wondering if tomorrow would be the day Ryan was going to propose. When he showed up in the morning with a camera guy, my suspicions were roused, but not about anything more than a proposal. It was almost comic relief when Ryan told the ladies at the hotel that he was proposing. This completely threw me off. Ryan is normally so romantic, and I couldn't believe that he would just tell those random women that he was proposing before actually going through with it. I was confused and eager to find out what was going on, but I trusted Ryan, and I went along with his plan without any hesitation.

It was only minutes later that Ryan told me for the first time that he loved me. Half of me was so happy that I wanted to burst out of my skin, but the funny thing is that the other half of me thought it sounded completely normal. I knew what those words meant to him, and I thought, *He just said it. This is it.* Before I could fully process that, he was proposing. The moment I'd been waiting for and thinking about for so long was finally here, and it didn't feel real. The ring he slid on my finger was more beautiful than any ring I'd ever imagined wearing, and I was completely overwhelmed.

Ryan grabbed my hand and started walking me closer to the hotel. I didn't understand why he was rushing me; I just wanted to savor the moment! But then he introduced me to the hotel's catering manager, and I knew something else was going on. He asked me, "Remember when you said you wanted to get engaged and married on the same day? What would we need to have here to do that?" I mumbled, "My family," feeling like I was in a trance. Ryan nodded. "Yeah, we'd need a few people here to do that. Well, the question isn't, 'Will you marry me,'" he continued. "The question is, "Will you marry me today?'" Ryan opened the door to the hotel and I saw one hundred of our closest friends and family members standing there, shouting, "TODAY!"

This moment has taken me almost a year to fully process. It was the single most exhilarating thing I'd ever experienced, and I felt so overwhelmed with love that I wanted to burst. For the first thirty seconds or so, I assumed that all these people had flown to Miami just to see us get engaged. But as I looked around the room and my eyes slowly focused on not only our parents and siblings and closest friends, but also cousins, mentors, and friends who lived far away and we hadn't seen in months, I realized that all these people hadn't flown here for any proposal. This was going down *today*.

Later in the book you'll read all about the five years between the first date Ryan and I went on and our engagement/wedding day. The main obstacle we faced during that time was my mother's disapproval of our relationship. This caused us to break up and take breaks, and even after we were back together and talking about getting married, I didn't know if my mother would ever approve. This had weighed on me for five years, and I felt happy when I saw my mother standing there in the hotel, but when I saw the *approval* on her face, I was amazed. It was an answer to prayer in the flesh, a complete full-circle moment indicating that whatever happened that day and on the days that followed, God had already answered two of my greatest prayers—marrying Ryan and having my mother approve. I felt as though I was standing in the middle of a miracle. God hadn't only brought my mother there that day, but he'd changed her heart toward my relationship with Ryan, and that was huge.

After I hugged my mom and cried more than a few tears, Ryan and I were separated as we circulated among the guests. When we reconnected a little later, it felt amazing and surreal. Ryan thanked everyone for coming and asked a friend of ours to lead us in two worship songs since none of this would have been possible without God. As she sang and played her guitar, my mind clicked back to the moment on the plane when I wrote about how grateful I was for God's blessings. This was the first time I'd seen a man go so completely out of his way and so far out of his comfort zone to make something happen for the woman he loved, and that woman was me.

There wasn't a lot of time to sit around and soak up all that love. Ryan and I immediately went to the city hall so we could get legally hitched without much fanfare, and then we went back to the hotel. Ryan had flown in my favorite makeup artist and hairstylist, and we went upstairs with my mom, godsisters, and besties for some fun, much-needed girl time while we got ready. A big storm that had been brewing outside had gotten worse throughout the day, and we had to decide whether to chance it and plan to have the wedding outside or do it inside. Ryan left it up to me, and I made the decision to just do it inside. At that point, I didn't care if it was inside, outside, or in the hotel room—I just wanted to marry Ryan Leak.

WHY WE WORK

Ryan

When I proposed to Amanda that morning, the sun was shining, but a storm had picked up speed throughout the day and eventually got so bad that they had to block off the street to the hotel. Cars were literally under water. It wasn't just a storm; it was a monsoon! My best friend's wife didn't make it to the wedding since the road was completely flooded, and we had to push the wedding back an hour because it was taking everyone so long to get there. The reception was supposed to be across the street, but the bridge to the other side was flooded and we had to move the whole party just a few hours before the wedding. Despite all this, when I saw Amanda walking down the aisle, it felt too good to be true.

Amanda and I know why we work. It's not just because we share the same moral values, because we're attracted to each other, or because we have fun on dates. Jesus Christ is what makes us tick, what makes us go. Whenever we thought about a hypothetical wedding, we said that the thing that was most important to us was that the guests at our wedding would sense something special, and that something special would be the presence of God.

In the middle of the wedding, my eleven-year-old niece came up to my brother, tapped him on the shoulder, and said, "Daddy, I want this." When I heard this, her words became one of the highlights of the entire day because I don't think she meant simply that she wanted a surprise wedding. My niece saw a guy who was willing to put all the chips on the table for a girl. She got a front-row seat to godly love, and I'm so glad she recognized it when she saw it. Not only my niece, but every girl out there deserves to be cherished and loved at the highest level. I hope our story serves as one small example of what all women truly deserve.

WE'LL SPEND OUR LIVES TRYING

Amanda

On the day of our engagement and wedding, I had no idea exactly how much work had gone into planning everything. Over the course of the day, Ryan told me a little bit about some of the challenges he'd faced, and I had a million more questions for him, but my focus that day wasn't on the planning. It was on being present in the moment and adjusting my mind-set, not only to getting used to being engaged, but also preparing to be all about our marriage.

On our honeymoon, my mind was finally clear, and I asked Ryan to tell me everything. As we sat on the beach and Ryan shared the details of everything he'd done—the planning, the saving, the stress, and the ups and downs—I couldn't believe it. I can't say it made me love Ryan any more than I already did because our love isn't contingent on that sort of thing, but it certainly brought my appreciation for him to a whole new level.

More than anything, knowing what Ryan was willing to do for me makes me want to spend our entire marriage making him feel as loved and valued as he made me feel that day. I don't know if that's even possible, but I am determined to spend my life trying.

This is our story. It's unique to Ryan and me, and we know it's not your story. That's okay. This book is full of stories from our dating relationship and some from our marriage, but this book isn't really about us. It's about you, the relationship you want, and the choices you can make to help you create one beautiful, unique, and inspiring love story of your very own.

One Question to Ask Yourself: When your grandkids sit on your lap decades from now and ask about how you and your spouse met, what story do you want to tell them?

One Thing to Remember: Nothing is impossible with God (see Matthew 19:26).

One Thing to Work On: Pray and ask God to help you read this book with an open heart.

2

Why You're Single

Sometimes I wish everyone were single like me—a simpler life in many ways! But celibacy is not for everyone any more than marriage is. God gives the gift of the single life to some, the gift of the married life to others.

—1 Corinthians 7:7, MSG

MAKING THE MOST OF YOUR SINGLE SEASON

Ryan

Before Amanda and I got married, I was in eleven weddings. Yes, you read that right—eleven. Every time, I was pumped to be there for the groom and celebrate with him, but over the course of the day the conversation somehow always turned to the single people who were present. At some point during the festivities, I'd end up in line for the buffet with the groom's father or taking pictures with the groom himself when he'd turn to me and ask, "What's going on with *you*? Why are you still single?" The women were no better. Every bridesmaid and auntie wanted to set me up with someone, and I felt like I needed to have a "good" answer to explain why I was single and why I had dared to show up at this wedding alone.

Our culture provides us with a picture of singleness that's so negative we're left to search for a reason why we've been cursed with the "disease." Are you still single because you've done something wrong? Are you being punished for some reason, or are you simply unworthy of marriage? The answer is no. In reality, your singleness is not a curse or a punishment. Your singleness is a gift. It's an opportunity. God has chosen to give you this gift of singleness for a reason, and it is up to you to accept this gift and make the most of it.

So many people sit in their singleness bitterly or spend all their time and money searching for the "one," instead of taking the opportunity to enjoy all the good things about their current season. I have a friend named Stacey who spent $250 a month on various online dating subscriptions. Now, I have nothing at all against online dating, and I know that nearly a third of all married couples met online, but to me this seemed excessive. I asked her, "Do you know what you could do with $250 a month if you decided to be purposeful with it?" I did some quick math. "That adds up to $3,000 a year." Instead of spending that money on online dating, Stacey could have gone on a mission trip and taken a friend with her, she could have simply given it to charity, or she could have bought lunch for a coworker once a week.

What if Stacey used that money to encourage somebody? We're all one compliment away from having the confidence to do exactly what God has designed us to do. Stacey could have used that money to help somebody fulfill her destiny, and I can almost guarantee this would have done more for her dating life than all those online subscriptions combined. I suggested that Stacey cancel her subscriptions and ask God what he wanted her to do with the money, knowing that if she became a light in this world, people would inevitably start talking about her character instead of something superficial in her online profile.

Not that I fantasize or dream about being single again, but if I could go back to that season, I would do even more. I would backpack across Europe at least once. I would find the places on this planet that are the worst of the worst and give a week of my life to shine a light there. Ask yourself this: What do you want to be known for? What story do you want to tell your kids and your grandkids? Singleness is a great opportunity to be a story, to tell a story, and to write a story. In the Bible, there are plenty of examples of single people accomplishing great things, starting with Jesus himself. What can you use this season of your life to achieve?

You can't control when Mr. or Miss Right will walk in the door, when your boyfriend will propose, or when your girlfriend will agree that you're the one. In 1 Corinthians 7:6–9, the Bible says that God gives the gift of a single life to some and the gift of a married life to others. It's not up to you to decide which one God will give you. The one thing you can control is whether or not you'll be ready to receive the gift God has in store for you. If you haven't met the one yet, do you want that person to show up and find someone who's been sitting around waiting for life to start or someone who's been busy living life to the fullest, being true to yourself, and acting as a messenger of God? You only have today, so give today everything you have. Your life will speak for itself, and when your future partner does arrive, he or she can choose to be a part of your story.

Your single season provides so many opportunities for you to learn about yourself, grow, and prepare to bring your best self to your relationship. Here are a few ways you can start to make the most of your single season today:

Live Your Dreams and Discover Your Passions

In my early twenties, I had the idea that marriage was restrictive. I prayed that I would get married one day, but I also knew that I'd have a lot less free time when I did, so I made a list of dreams and goals and set about accomplishing them. I saw the Lakers play at Staples Center in Los Angeles; I traveled to New York and learned that it was a bomb city to visit but that I'd never want to live there; I sat down with producers in Hollywood and found that while I love movies, the entertainment industry wasn't for me in that particular season. I also devoted myself to really knowing and understanding the Bible, not just so I could be a better speaker when I preach, but to better understand this phenomenal and divine Book that was written for me. If the Bible is, at minimum, a solid moral compass for human living, I wanted to make sure I knew how to navigate through its directions.

Make a list of dreams and goals for yourself, and start checking them off one by one. No, this isn't always easy. If you really want to do something, it will cost you; but don't use that as an excuse. Instead, ask yourself this pivotal question: *What am I willing to give up for this dream?* Every successful person in the world has one thing in common— sacrifice. Put in the work, do favors for others, and ask for some in return. Be strong. By the time you start a relationship, I pray you won't have any regrets. I had to eat peanut butter and jelly every day for six months to pay for a plane ticket to LA, but I would be so full of regret today if I'd never seen my Lakers play in person.

While you're busy accomplishing your dreams, take this opportunity to discover what you're passionate about. One good question to ask yourself is what you enjoy spending money on and where you're willing to skimp. Some people will buy thrift-store clothes and then splurge on dinner at a nice restaurant. For Amanda and me, food doesn't hold a lot of value. We're happy to go to Chipotle and instead spend our money on manicures (her), NBA games (me), and giving to others (both of us).

It's important to discover your passions before getting into a relationship. If you don't know what you're passionate about, you may find someone you like and start to become the person you think she wants you to be instead of becoming the one God has called you to be. Have you known people who started dating someone and suddenly had a bunch of new hobbies, only to snap back to the person they used to be as soon as the relationship ended? You don't want to wake up in a few years and realize you don't really enjoy any of the things you and the person you're dating do together. Now is your time to figure out who you are and what is important to you so you can find someone who values the real you.

Fail Early

Once you have a list of a few dreams you'd like to accomplish, start trying to make them happen. Maybe you'll succeed and maybe you'll fail. Either way, it's better to find out sooner than later. Don't wait until you're married with kids to find out why you'll never play for the Yankees, star in a movie, or run your own company. You have less to lose and more to gain now. Go ahead and get kicked out of acting class, get cut from *American Idol,* and get rejected from law school. Train for a marathon and see how far you get. Fail as early as you can, and take good notes. This is the only way to learn what you need to do in order to succeed on the next go 'round.

Understand Your Wiring

We recently met Melissa at a young-adult event. She got up and spoke about how hard it was for her to trust men because of her relationship with her father. Her mom raised her; her dad would call her from time to time and promise to do things with her or buy her things, but he always broke those promises. This past summer Melissa was enrolled in her last semester of college, but she didn't have enough money to pay the tuition. Her dad asked her, "How much do you need?" When she told him, he promised her several times that he'd put that amount in her account, but he never did. Melissa had to drop out and get a job waitressing instead of finishing her degree.

The one person who was supposed to instill confidence in Melissa failed to do so, and now she has a very hard time trusting others, especially men. In a relationship, whenever she's let down in any way, she immediately reverts to "You're just like my dad."

After hearing Melissa's story, Amber spoke up. "I can relate to that," she said. "My dad did the same thing to me and my brother. A few times he told us he was going to take us on a trip. We'd pack our bags and be out on the front porch waiting for him, but he never showed up." Amber shared how this has created trust issues for her. "If I text a guy and he doesn't respond within five minutes," she said, "I go right back to the porch."

We've all gone through things that can take us back to the porch, and they're not always simple or easy to fix. But how great is it that they were able to share their stories in community? Now these girls have the most important thing they need in order to heal—awareness.

Self-improvement is a never-ending story, but your single season serves as a time when you can work on yourself with fewer responsibilities. Take an honest look in the mirror and start to evaluate yourself and your readiness for marriage. Are you ready to bring your best to a relationship? Would you want to marry you with all your insecurities and issues? This is your opportunity to get to know yourself on a deep level—not just your dreams and passions, but also the wiring underneath it all that makes you *you*. Have you been through personal counseling to understand the dynamics of the family you come from? Do you have people in your life who are guiding you? Think of this time of singleness as a high school AP class, a higher-level class that lets you show up at college with credit already in the bank. In this case, the hard work you do now will allow you to show up for marriage with extra credit, a full step ahead of someone who didn't take the time to get to know himself or herself first. This is why you're single—to get that credit that will pay dividends in this season and the next one.

Becoming Whole

Amanda

I learned to be a confident single woman from my mom. She grew up in a traditional Hispanic household with protective parents, and because she was shy and somewhat sheltered, my dad was the first guy she'd ever dated. Her father wasn't very fond of him, but they continued dating, and when she was twenty-one, she got pregnant with my brother. My mom and dad were married when she was a few months pregnant, and two years later I came along. My mom will admit that she didn't know my dad as well as she could have before the wedding; she also didn't know herself yet. She was extremely smart and hardworking, but because of her upbringing she was also a little naive. At that point she hadn't gone to college or really experienced much of life.

Meanwhile, my dad had grown up believing that in a marriage the husband should control the home. His dad died when he was a teenager, and he developed a lot of anger issues that he never really dealt with. He suppressed his anger for a while, but over the years it came out when he yelled at my mom or acted aggressively with my brother and me. As I got older, my mom started going to church with my "godfamily," a local family we'd grown extremely close to. I call my godsisters "my sisters" because we're just as closely connected as family. This relationship was great for my mom, but it made things worse between her and my dad. He hated the fact that she was going to church. He began to get more physical, not only with her, but also with me and my brother.

My mom felt trapped in the marriage. She tried to make it work for years because divorce wasn't an option in the culture she came from.

Eventually she found out that my dad had been cheating on her, and they were divorced shortly after that.

Once she was a single mom, my mother started working two jobs to pay the bills. We struggled a bit, but she always provided for us, and God blessed us in a million small ways that made life easier—mostly by bringing generous and kind people into our lives. Then when I was in seventh grade, my mom decided to go back to school to get an associate's degree in computer engineering, something she knew nothing about. Once she got her associate's degree, she went on to get a BA degree. She did all this while working full time to support my brother and me. She worked all day, made us dinner every single night, and then stayed up until the middle of the night studying just to do it all over again the next day. I remember being impressed with this at the time, but today I am in awe of her strength and the strength of all single mothers.

My mom has always been beautiful. After the divorce, she had plenty of opportunities to date—that was never a struggle! I remember asking her if she'd ever date again, and her response was, "I have things I need to accomplish first, to raise you and your brother and finish school." She wasn't letting anything get in her way, and she told me that she'd consider dating only after she'd reached those goals. During the next several years, she didn't date anyone, and she was obviously confident about her status. Not once did I see her moping about being single or complaining about raising us kids alone. Instead, I saw what a resilient and completely independent woman looked like.

I didn't know this at the time, but my mom told me recently that she intentionally stayed single for so long to give my brother and me a chance to heal from the past without any distractions. She knew how much we'd suffered from my dad's negative behaviors, and she wanted to bring us up in the ways of the Lord without the influence of another male on our family.

Because of my mom's attitude toward being single, I never thought of it as something negative. In my house, independence was something to celebrate. Growing up without much of a relationship with my dad, I was also pretty shy around guys. I had some really awesome guy friends in high school, but if any of them expressed interest beyond friendship, I began to feel uncomfortable and responded by distancing myself. Still, I was curious about what a relationship would look like for me. There were many days during my train ride home from school in Chicago when I'd look out the window and wonder what it would be like to be in a relationship with someone I loved.

I found out after I graduated from high school and started dating a guy who seemed amazing. Well, he was amazing compared to the guys I'd known before, but I soon realized that I had only a small circle to compare him to. I'd been around people in only a few settings, mostly church and high school. This guy was great in the context of what I knew, but what else was out there?

I didn't want to repeat my mom's mistake by getting into a relationship with anyone before I fully knew myself, so I decided to focus on me for one year with no distractions. I moved to Atlanta to intern at a church leadership program and spent that year traveling, learning, and crossing a bunch of things off my bucket list. I wanted to become whole. My mission for that year was to "Just go. Just do." And I did.

In fact, I was so busy going and doing that when Corey, the church's worship pastor, told me that his brother Ryan was coming to Atlanta for the summer and hinted that he thought we'd be a good match, I completely brushed it off. Even when Corey's wife, Julie, who'd become a close and trusted friend, said, "Hold on—I can really see the two of you together," I smiled and simply said, "No, thanks." Everyone at the church knew Ryan because they were part of the ministry he'd grown up with in Rockford, Illinois, which had recently moved to Atlanta. They all talked about how amazing Ryan was, but my year of being single wasn't up yet, and I wasn't interested.

A few weeks after Corey and Julie told me about Ryan, he showed up in Atlanta. I was running around the church that morning, trying to prepare for an event for junior high students that was taking place that night. As I walked from one room of the church toward the main sanctuary, I saw Corey standing in the hallway with a little grin on his face. Before I could ask him what that was all about, Ryan came around the corner. I immediately froze. Everything about him seemed to match the way I always pictured my future husband, from his tall, athletic build and genuine smile to his swagger! For the first time in my life, a boy literally stopped me in my tracks, and I just stood there watching the confident, down-to-earth way he carried himself. There was something almost familiar about Ryan, and before we even spoke I felt completely comfortable in his presence. He had an infectious joy and a smile like nothing could get him down. It seemed that life for him— and around him—was fun. And it is.

I was definitely intrigued by Ryan, but I had another month before the internship program ended, and I wasn't going to break the promise I'd made to myself. For that entire month, Ryan and I didn't date. We never even spoke! Corey and Julie had told Ryan that I'd made a promise to myself not to date until the internship was over, and he honored this from the beginning. He didn't even ask me out until I'd graduated. And in turn I became more fascinated than ever by him and appreciative of his obvious respect for my wishes.

In order to become whole, my goals for that year in Atlanta were to heal from the past, make memories, and learn more about who I was. I knew that I wouldn't be ready for a relationship until I did these things, and I think the same is true for every single person out there.

Heal from the Past

Throughout that year, I worked a lot with mentors at the church to heal from the "daddy issues" that had kept me from feeling completely comfortable around guys in the past. I'm so glad I took that time to heal before I met Ryan, but in retrospect I realize that I could have done even more. Though I'd come a long way, I never really dealt with the dysfunction in my parents' marriage that caused them to split up nor fully healed from the actual divorce. Instead, I absorbed the message that when there are issues in a relationship, it's okay to just shut down and walk away. This became my coping mechanism. Years later when Ryan and I were dating and I got upset with him, I'd just take off and go home, thinking this was better than blowing up and starting a screaming match.

Ryan and I were on the same page about most things from day one, so we didn't argue all that much, but we're still human. We had our share of disagreements and unmet expectations. Whenever I felt I was being misunderstood or got overwhelmed, I'd grab my keys and purse and head out the door. On the way home, I'd replay every moment of the disagreement in my head, feeling distraught and full of anger. This happened until one day when I was driving home with smoke coming out of my ears. Suddenly I saw myself driving away from someone I cared about and visualized myself doing this in the future as a wife and mother.

In that moment, I felt the Lord place a realization on my heart, and I saw that I was doing exactly what I'd seen my dad do a million times when I was growing up. Without thinking, I'd let that seep into my relationship with Ryan, and if I didn't stop now, I would end up projecting the same behavior onto my kids one day. This moment of clarity was all I needed to begin healing and consciously change my behavior.

If you keep hitting a wall in relationships as I did or have started to notice a pattern in your behavior that you just can't seem to shake or explain, maybe it's time to reflect on the learned behaviors from your past. If you're having trouble getting to the root cause of your issue, seek God and ask him, "What are my blind spots?" Deep down, you might already know, and if you spend time with yourself and with God, the answer will be revealed. When it is, face it head on, and allow Him to heal you.

Create Memories

Once you've spent some time healing from your past, it's time to focus on filling your life with positive memories and experiences. The best way I've found to do this is by traveling, whether it's across an ocean or simply across the street. Seeing different ways of life will help you grow spiritually and give you a more holistic worldview. It's so refreshing to get outside your little bubble in your small portion of the world to see how much life exists beyond you and yours! How will you ever learn what's important to you if you know only one way of doing things?

I recently met a dad who was struggling with his teenage daughter. She had a typical teen attitude and was spending too much time obsessing over a guy who was bad for her. Her dad said sadly, "Her whole life is consumed by high school gossip and this boy." To my surprise, another father spoke up and said, "Well, that makes sense. What else has she seen in the world besides her suburban high school?"

This took the girl's father aback, but when he went home and thought about it, he realized the other dad was right. He and his wife hadn't exposed their daughter to anything else. That summer, he decided to take his daughter on a trip to Africa where they volunteered at an orphanage. This experience completely changed the girl's life. She felt more fulfilled than ever working there and decided that kind of work is what she wants to do for the rest of her life.

Think about sitting across from a guy or girl and asking what that person has been doing for the past year. Would you rather date the person who says, "Same old, same old," or the one who's full of stories about traveling and seeing and doing new things? Don't let yourself become the person who's stuck doing the same old, same old. If you're single and, looking back over your life, you realize that you haven't made many lifelong memories, don't worry—you're in the perfect position for God to rock your world and take you on a journey. Just ask Him to!

Some of my best memories were made when I was serving others, from trips to Uganda and Guatemala to serving the poor in New York and my home city of Chicago. Why not start there? You could travel to a remote village or just visit a neighbor and find out if there's a way you can serve that person. You never know where a simple trip down the block can lead until you go there.

Learn Who You Are

Healing from the past and expanding your worldview will help you become a whole person who knows who you are. Can a relationship between two people who don't know who they are last? Maybe, but I don't believe it will thrive, and for you we want more than a mediocre relationship. It's true confidence and contentment that will help you find a partner who celebrates the real you and encourages you to be the best possible version. And of course you can find true confidence and contentment only when you have a deep understanding of who you are.

Don't worry that making your single life a priority will keep your future spouse away. The opposite is actually true. The more committed you are to your own life, the better chance you have of entering a healthy relationship. You could meet the one today, but if you're not full of purpose and busy making the most of your opportunities, will you be the one he or she is looking for? Make sure your future spouse walks into your life when you're at your best and living every moment to the fullest instead of waiting for your life to start when he or she appears.

One Question to Ask Yourself: What can God do with your single season?

One Thing to Remember: Your singleness is a gift, not a disease.

One Thing to Work On: Write down a list of goals that you want to accomplish during this season.

3

Getting Serious

Be very careful, then, how you live—not as unwise but as wise, making the most of every opportunity, because the days are evil.

—Ephesians 5:15–16

RIGHT AT THE START

Amanda

Shortly before I met Ryan, I found myself alone in the chapel of the church where I was interning. I sat in the pew and thought about how happy and content I was with my single life. I was doing exactly what I wanted to be doing, and I felt incredibly grateful and blessed. As I prayed, I told God that I wouldn't mind staying single forever, but if he did have someone for me, I hoped it would be someone I could change the world with.

By submitting my future relationship and marriage to God, I set myself free. There was no need for me to worry or try to control the outcome, and when things got confusing later, I had faith that everything was happening according to God's plan. As soon as I spoke those words to God, I knew I was accountable. If I'd met an average guy who would have been content with a simple life, he would be God's best for someone else, but God would know that I was settling for someone who had no interest in changing the world with me. Don't get me wrong: there's absolutely nothing wrong with a simple life. It just wasn't in line with my desires. And if I settled for that, He would know that I wasn't letting things unfold according to His plan.

Being intentional with God about your relationship before it even begins is the best thing you can do to lay the foundation for a healthy marriage. Intentionality means completely submitting your future, your sexuality, and all your relationships to God. When I did this, I was able to move forward with confidence. I didn't have to worry about which guy was the right one for me. Instead, I was certain I would know it was right when I heard God's voice. I had no idea when or how the right person would come into my life, but I trusted God with it.

At the time, I didn't put too much thought into the wording of wanting someone "I could change the world with." All I knew was that I didn't want to settle. I wanted to not only grow with another person, but also to thrive, and that was my way of describing it. A few months later, Ryan and I were on our first date. As we sat across from each other, I casually asked him what he wanted to do with his life, and his answer almost left me speechless. He took a moment, grinned, and said, "I want to change the world."

Naturally, I replied, "Oh my gosh, you're my future husband!" Just kidding; I played it cool. I filed this information in my mental storage cabinet and followed up with a few questions about exactly how he proposed to change the world. Was this a sign from God that Ryan was the one? Maybe. But it definitely helped me see that Ryan and I were both up for a challenge and wanted the same things.

How will you recognize the person God has meant for you if you're not intentional with Him? Take some time to think about your purpose for dating. Do you want someone you can change your community with, serve God with, or change the world with? Set your intention now, and then run from everyone else until you meet the one!

I once heard Pastor Mike Hayes of Covenant Church in Dallas say, "You can buy the wrong car, and it's not a destiny-altering thing. You can buy a house that wasn't worth it and sell it and buy another. All of these things can be changed and will have a slight impact in the lifetime scheme of things. But who you choose to marry will have the greatest impact on your destiny." So when I say run, I'm serious. *Run!* Run from anything and anyone that is less than what God has intended for you.

Our friend John once told Ryan and me, "Be very specific when you pray. That way, when it happens you'll know it was God." Pray specifically and pray big. The culture we live in today encourages us to talk about our problems more than we pray about problems. We'd rather sit down with a friend over coffee and talk about the things that bother us than sit in a chair in our house alone, praying to what feels like a ceiling. But connecting with the One who wrote your story and planned your entire destiny will take you further than any pep talk you could receive from a friend. On the path to becoming the one, prayer is vastly underrated.

STEP INTO LOVE, DON'T FALL

Ryan

Even the act of falling in love can and should be intentional. You'll never find the words "fall in love" in the Bible, because the love God shows us isn't an accident or something you can just "fall" into. Think about it this way: if you can fall in love accidentally, can't you just as easily fall out? Marriage is a commitment, not a decision you make when all the stars perfectly align. Too many people decide they've fallen in or out of love based on a temporary feeling, and this leads to so much heartache and confusion. But you can take steps to make love an intentional part of your relationship before it even begins, rather than something that you randomly fall into or out of.

Before I met Amanda I hadn't done a ton of dating, and the few relationships I'd been in hadn't helped me and hadn't really hurt me. With Amanda, it felt special before it even started, and I wanted to do things differently. I believed I had found a great girl and this was an opportunity to do things right from the beginning. I'd actually planned an extravagant first date that included Jet Skis and a steak dinner, but right before I picked her up, I decided to pull the plug on all that and just show up as the raw, real version of me. Sure, I'm big on grand gestures, but not every day. I wanted Amanda to see me on an average day, not necessarily a spectacular day. The difference this time was that I wasn't trying to impress her. I was trying to connect with her.

For me, intentionality meant coming into the relationship with all my cards on the table. I never played poker with Amanda. Instead, I was upfront about my intentions from the very beginning. "I don't know what's going to happen," I told her. "We may end up dating or we may end up being friends. But if we're going to be friends, let's be the best friends we can be."

When we did start dating, my intention of making things great from the beginning started to spill over into my other relationships. I suddenly saw where I'd been acting without intention and was able to become a better brother and a better friend to my male friends. I hadn't expected that to happen, but it was a great bonus. And because I'd been so intentional with Amanda, I trusted that God could make our relationship happen if He wanted to. I was no longer biased, and I was able to live and enjoy my life exactly as it was.

CREATE YOUR PERFECT MATE

Besides prayer, the best way I know to be intentional about finding the right person is to create a list of what you're looking for in a mate. Have you ever stopped to think about what specific qualities you want your future spouse to have? I'm not talking about looks, though physical attraction is important and shouldn't be disregarded. I'm talking about the deeper, more lasting traits.

Take a moment to write down a list of qualities that you want in a partner; really push yourself to go deeper than you ever have before. This is your one chance to create your dream partner, at least on paper, so really go for it. What are the qualities that will make this person not

only a good date or a good girlfriend or boyfriend right now, but someone you want to be with in the long term? I couldn't have put it in
words at the time, but one thing I instantly felt with Amanda was safe.
Safety may not be sexy, but it's essential in the long run. Colossians 3:12
tells us, "Therefore, as God's chosen people, holy and dearly loved,
clothe yourselves with compassion, kindness, humility, gentleness and
patience." Traits like honesty, kindness, selflessness, patience, submission to authority, modesty, courage, diligence, faithfulness, respectful-
ness, wisdom, and commitment to Christ may not be sexy on a date, but
they look great on a husband or wife and amazing on a mom or dad.

This exercise is so valuable because if you don't have a standard of
what you're looking for, you're more likely to settle for anything. So
many people believe that as long as they have someone they can post a
photo with on social media, their lives are on the right track, but the
truth is that you'll be far worse off settling for the wrong person than
you will be staying single. Everyone's dream guy or girl will not be iden-
tical. Take the time to define what the one is like for *you* while making
sure to pray about what God would have for you.

Try to focus on the qualities you want in a partner rather than the
qualities you *don't* want. This will keep you from simply reacting to the
past and thinking that all you need is an antidote to the person you
were with before. One girl I know dated a guy who was broke. Every
time they went out, they had to split the bill. They eventually broke up,
and the next guy she dated had a lot of money. "It's awesome," she told
me. My response was, "Compared to what?"

Once you're happy with your list of desired qualities, read it over
again, but this time, instead of fantasizing about finding another person

who possesses all these great qualities, I want you to ask yourself which of them *you* have. Yes, it's incredibly important to know what traits you'd like to find in a partner, but it's just as important to make sure you are living up to these same standards. You must embody the qualities you want to find in a mate. This is the only way to enter a healthy relationship and to keep it balanced long into the future.

We all paint a picture in our minds of what it's like to be in a relationship. In this picture, you're holding hands with your dream date. He's tall, athletic, kind, and generous. He can talk about his feelings, laughs at your jokes that aren't funny, buys you flowers, loves your friends, treats you like a queen, and makes you laugh. She's hot. She never gossips, dresses nice, thinks you're Superman, isn't emotional, never makes you talk about your feelings, loves sports, watches ESPN, and doesn't mind when you go out with your buddies. That's all good, but now take a look at yourself in this picture. So many times we build the whole image around the assumption that we are already a dream guy or girl who's worthy of the other person in the picture.

Switch your thinking from what you deserve to what the person you want to be with deserves and needs. You can't change the person you're dating, but you can work on you. It's only when you start focusing on creating the best version of you in the picture that you can start painting everything else. As you look at your list of desired qualities, evaluate yourself honestly. You want to find someone who inspires you? Great. Who did you inspire today? You can't expect to receive what you do not provide. If you lie, why would an honest person want to be with you? If you act selfishly, why would a giving person choose you? I can't believe how many times a guy will privately (and sometimes rudely) tell me that he wishes his girlfriend would lose weight, when his own feet haven't stepped inside the doors of a gym in years.

It can be difficult to evaluate yourself with complete honesty, so I recommend taking your list to a few trusted friends and asking them to be straight with you about which of these qualities you already possess and which ones you need to work on. I have a few close friends I call "The Committee." I consider them the board of directors of my life, and I run all my important decisions by them. If your friends tell you that you already have all these traits, keep working every day to live up to them. But if there are a few you aren't living up to, you need to start striving to embody these traits today. Remember, your job is not to be perfect, but to be the very best version of you that you can be. You can't find the one until you become the one.

SETTLING FOR LESS

Amanda

Settling is the opposite of intentionality. It's committing yourself to someone you don't experience a true connection with for one reason or another. The most critical thing to know is that if you do settle, this is the way it's going to stay. Don't expect things to magically change once you get married. If you choose to marry someone who's nice and wholesome but who you don't have a lot in common with, getting married won't make you suddenly have more in common (other than a shared address). You will still be the same person, and so will your spouse. The only difference will be that now you're committed to staying together and loving each other for life.

When I was in college, there were lounges in each of the male and female dorms. Sometimes when a guy was interested in a girl, he'd come to the female lounge to hang out on the couch and watch TV with her. My friends and I called this "couch dating." It required zero effort from the guys, and of course most of those relationships never went anywhere. Of course, there's nothing wrong with a simple date where you watch a movie and order takeout, but if that's all you're doing, there's a problem. It's all about intentionality.

If you're looking for an amazing love story and not just a couch date, be careful not to send the message that a potential mate doesn't have to make any effort with you. Don't accept zero effort from a guy in the beginning of a relationship and assume that things will change down the road. I hate to say it, but a guy who gets away with zero effort dating in the beginning isn't likely to suddenly start making an effort once you get serious about each other or even after you're married. It was clear to Ryan from the beginning that I wasn't dating him just to date. I was busy and joyful and living my life with a clear purpose, and he knew that he could either join the party or not. Either way, I would have been fine. If Ryan hadn't been intentional about pursuing me, I never would have stayed in Atlanta to spend time with him, and he knew that. This set the tone and pace of our relationship from the beginning.

Think about what signals you're sending out to the people you date. Are you so wrapped up in the layers of your full and happy life that it takes a little bit of work to get to you, or are you available for anyone and anything? The more fulfilling your single life is, the less likely you'll be to give in to loneliness. I've seen so many friends end up in relationships that are headed nowhere, and while I completely sympathize, I also wish they hadn't settled for "couch dating" in the first place.

Whether or not to settle is your choice, but when you know that God has someone you'll connect with on a much deeper and more meaningful level, why would you? Following are some of the most common reasons I've heard for people to settle.

"I Don't Believe I Deserve Better"

Some people settle because they don't believe they deserve to experience a true godly love. If you don't believe that God has someone for you or that you even deserve this type of love, then your focus needs to be on issues that are more critical than whether or not to settle. Don't even worry about being in a relationship right now. There's another priority, and that is you. Pause wherever you are—bookmark this page—and lay down the idea of marriage and dating. You can come back to that later. Until you heal and develop a positive feeling of self-worth, a healthy relationship or marriage is completely out of the question. Seek the help of a mentor, pastor, or counselor to heal yourself so that you can enter a relationship as a whole, healthy person. Don't be ashamed about asking for help. I had to do the same thing, and there are tons of people out there who should be doing this but choose not to. Facing your issues and taking the time to heal puts you a step ahead, not behind.

Being off balance about what you think you deserve leads not only to settling but also to not realizing what you have when you have it. A friend of ours recently told Ryan and me that his girlfriend keeps telling him that she doesn't deserve him. Why does she think that? Because she's imperfect? Well, all of us are. God crafted you with a certain amount of grace, and you deserve His best for you. Of course, that person will be imperfect in his or her own way, too. If God brings you a good thing, don't spend your time worrying about whether or not you "deserve" him or her, and instead focus on taking the best care of what He's blessed you with.

"I Don't Believe It Exists"

If a feeling of self-worth isn't an issue for you but you still have doubts about whether or not a happy marriage is possible, maybe you grew up witnessing an unhealthy picture of love and marriage. After witnessing my parents' toxic marriage, I was curious to find out if there was something better out there. I looked at other couples who seemed happy, from my third grade teacher to random people at the grocery store. I grabbed little bits and pieces from each of them and used them to patch together my own image of what marriage could and should be instead of settling for a mirror image of the unhealthy marriage I grew up in. Something powerful I've heard from a lot of pastors is, "Your world is not the world." There's so much more out there than anything you've personally seen or experienced. If your world has shown you a dark or negative version of marriage, actively seek another perspective. Maybe there's a happily married older couple who could serve as mentors or a counselor who can help you heal from what you've seen in the past and show you that there is something better out there.

"I Don't Want to Wait"

Other people settle because they're in such a rush that they assume whoever they happen to spend time with is the one for them. Have you ever noticed that when people get together as a group on a regular basis—at school, work, or church—they start to look at the members of the opposite sex in their group for the best option in the bunch? Pretty soon, they pick one and start to have "feelings" for that person. But does proximity really make someone the right person for you? The one you'll share a true connection with might be a world away or even a few years down the road. Sure, your future spouse might be at your school, workplace, or church, but he or she may very well not be.

When you meet someone and start developing feelings for this person, it's important not to let those feelings get ahead of your logic. Being intentional means filtering your emotions through your logic, not the other way around. One way to make sure you're doing this right is to slow down! I've seen some of my girlfriends meet a guy, develop feelings, and start picturing what their kids together would look like after knowing him for only a week! Then a month or so later, their feelings fade and they end up saying, "Eww, gross—what was I thinking?!" I tell them, "You weren't thinking, you were *feeling*."

Sure, you can develop crushes on people. There's nothing wrong with that. You just need to give yourself time to see whether those feelings will grow or fade. Keep it in the "friend" zone for five weeks or so, and then see what happens. I call this the "Five Week Rule." After about five weeks, you'll have a pretty clear idea of whether or not this person really deserves more of your time. If you jump into a relationship with someone right away, your feelings might override your logic. When your feelings are in charge, it becomes too easy to get swept away by a tidal wave of emotions and end up with someone who isn't right for you. The result is settling, even if that's not what it feels like at the moment. The Bible warns us in Jeremiah 17:9 that the heart can be deceptive. In James 1:5 we are told that God will give generously if we pray for wisdom. If we put our feelings in charge of major decisions, instead of wisdom and logic, they can too easily bulldoze right over the truth of the situation. Give it time to see if that person you have feelings for is worth settling—or striving—for.

One Question to Ask Yourself: What can you do to be more intentional about your relationships?

One Thing to Remember: You can't control when the person you'll marry will arrive on the scene, but you can work on yourself in the meantime.

One Thing to Work On: Write down a list of qualities you want to find in a mate and then ask yourself if you possess those qualities.

4

Overcoming Obstacles

> Therefore, since we are surrounded by such a great cloud of witnesses, let us throw off everything that hinders and the sin that so easily entangles. And let us run with perseverance the race marked out for us.
>
> —Hebrews 12:1

THRIVING UNDER PRESSURE

Amanda

Despite our fairy-tale wedding, Ryan and I have not had an easy love story. In fact, we went through a bumpy ride in order to become fully ready for each other. While it was painful at the time and I spent plenty of nights crying into my pillow, in retrospect I wouldn't take away the challenges we went through. God knew exactly what we needed to prepare for the marriage we share today, and our story illustrates one of our most valuable pieces of advice—hurdles in a relationship can either break you or make you. You can let obstacles destroy you and your relationship or view them as opportunities to really shine.

When we first met, Ryan and I still hadn't even spoken when I had to decide whether to stay in Atlanta for an extra week to spend time with him or head home to my mom's in Chicago as I had originally planned. I was a little bit nervous calling my mom to tell her about Ryan, but nothing could have prepared me for her reaction when I told her I was thinking about staying the extra week to hang out with him.

"No," she told me plainly. "You are supposed to be focusing on your program, not chasing after some boy."

"But my program is ending next week," I told her. "I kept my promise. And he's not just 'some boy.' He seems really special, and I want a chance to talk to him." I explained that I wasn't chasing after him at all. I was simply accepting his invitation to hang out and get to know each other. "Who knows if it will even become something?" I asked. "But I would like to give it a chance."

"No," she said again. "You can't change your plans for him. You'll end up throwing your dreams away to do whatever he wants. I won't allow it."

I hung up feeling completely distraught. I knew my mom was just trying to protect me. She would have done anything to keep me from making the same mistakes she made. But in this case, it didn't seem fair. I was turning twenty. I was an adult now, wasn't I? Didn't I have a right to start making my own decisions? I went over these questions a million times in my head. It may seem obvious if you grew up in a different culture, but it was hard for me to imagine going against my mother's wishes. For my entire life, I'd almost always done as she said.

Luckily, part of my work that year had been learning how to mentor junior high school students, and I'd done this by forming relationships with mentors of my own, a group of women at the church who encouraged me to talk out my decision-making process. They also knew Ryan through the ministry he'd grown up in, so they were able to tell me about his character and assure me that I could trust him. This helped me see that I wasn't doing any harm by staying in Atlanta and that I had to start trusting my intuition and the peace I felt about the situation. It was still a struggle for me, but I finally decided to go against my mother's wishes and stay in Atlanta for a few extra days.

On the day of my internship graduation, my stomach was filled with butterflies. I had been anticipating this day for months. It marked the start of a new chapter in my life, and I was ready for it. Oh, and I was finally going to talk to Ryan Leak! After getting my diploma, I ran into the bathroom to quickly freshen up. There was a Lakers game on that day that I knew Ryan and his brother Corey would be dying to watch, but I wanted to talk to Ryan first. I was fixing my hair in the mirror when Corey's three little daughters came running in and started pulling on my arm. I'd grown close to them that summer, and they called me *Titi,* the Spanish word for auntie. "Titi 'Manda!" they shouted, full of smiles and giggles.

"Yes, girlies?" I asked them. I could see the excitement on their sweet little faces.

Amiah, the oldest at seven, yelled, "Hurry! Our daddy wants to go watch the Lakers, but first Uncle Ryan has to tell you that he likes you!"

I stepped out of the bathroom and saw Ryan in the sanctuary looking for me. I walked right over to him. "Hi, I'm Ryan," he said, with a smile so big that it was almost a laugh.

"I'm Amanda," I replied.

"I know." I was trying to play it cool, but I seriously could not stop smiling. No other guy had ever made me blush like this! I usually tried to play it cool, act strong, and never let them see me sweat, but this Ryan Leak had me off my game. We already knew so much about each other that I felt completely comfortable with him even though we'd never spoken. "I'm excited to hang out tomorrow if you want to," Ryan said, and I nodded, completely smitten. "Me, too," I told him.

When he picked me up the next day, the first thing Ryan said was, "I'm gonna be totally honest with you. I usually like to have a plan, and I did come up with some things we could do today, but the timing didn't work and everything got all mixed up. But it helped me realize something," he continued, "I just want to be real with you, without all the bells and whistles that I usually try to pull off. Are you cool with just hanging out?"

I loved how upfront he was. Ryan wasn't putting on a show or trying to impress me, but he was still being intentional about getting to know me, and that made me like him even more. We spent the whole day driving around, listening to John Mayer, and eventually stopping at Wendy's. It may not sound romantic, but it was perfect. We talked about everything . . . and nothing at all. I felt completely comfortable with Ryan, like I'd known him forever, and I could feel the walls I'd built up around myself as a young girl slowly falling down.

At the end of the evening, Ryan asked if I wanted to get together again the next day. "I have a surprise for you," he said. When I said yes, he told me to bring twelve outfits. "What for?" I asked, already going through my closet in my mind. I'd have to borrow some outfits from my friends! "Can I get a hint?"

"Sure, I'll give you a hint," he told me, with a twinkle in his eye. "It takes a year to make a movie, but it only takes an hour to watch it." That night I went to my friends' apartment and told them, "I need you to put your cutest clothes in this bag right now!" When I told them what was going on, they all screamed with excitement as we started picking out outfits while trying to guess the surprise.

Ryan picked me up the next morning, and I threw my bag in the backseat as I asked, "So what do you have in mind today, Mr. Leak?" He told me, "I was thinking about how it feels like we've known each other forever—but what if we could make it look like we really have?" Over the course of the day, Ryan took me from one place to the next, and each time we changed clothes and took a picture with a disposable camera. Our stops included a music store, the airport, the ballpark, a carnival, and a furniture store that we staged to look like it was someone's apartment. At the end of the day, we got the pictures developed. Flipping through them, it looked like we'd gone on twelve different dates, as if we'd been a couple for a long time and had built a whole friendship together. And that's exactly how it felt to both of us, too.

This guy has set the bar, I thought to myself. I had never met anyone like him. He'd put so much thought into just one day, and by the end of it I felt 100 percent myself around him. This was the very first time I'd felt that way with a guy. I knew I didn't have to impress him or try to be someone I wasn't, and it was completely refreshing.

It was hard saying good-bye to Ryan at the end of that week, but it was time to go home, and I was excited to see what the future held for me and for us. When I got home, though, I was caught completely off guard by how upset my mom still was. "You disobeyed me," she said as soon as I walked into the house. Over the next few weeks, she made it clear that she disapproved of me talking to Ryan. She'd never even met him, yet she refused to give him a chance. Naturally, this infuriated me! But I knew how afraid she was that I would follow the same path she had. The culture I come from can also be very old-fashioned. The older generations would have it that I exclusively date and ultimately marry within our culture. Secretly, I wondered if part of the disapproval stemmed from the fact that Ryan is black, but this thought was too awful even to vocalize.

The next few months were the best and the worst for me. Ryan was at college in Minneapolis, but we continued getting to know each other long distance as if nothing had happened with my mom. We talked on the phone every night until three or four in the morning, never running out of things to say. Sometimes we'd fall asleep on the phone. (Corny, I know!) Ryan came to visit me twice in Chicago, and we talked less in person, sometimes just staring at each other in awe that we were finally together in the same city. In between his calls and visits, Ryan sent me cards, texts, e-mails, and little gifts to let me know he was thinking of me.

Meanwhile, I was feeling more confident than ever, not only because of the work I'd done that year in Atlanta, but because of Ryan. For the first time, I felt confident that I could be in a healthy relationship. My friends noticed this and didn't doubt it when I told them I thought I'd found "the one."

At the same time, my relationship with my mother was truly suffering. I prayed about it continuously but was still constantly torn, feeling as if I had to choose between Ryan and my mom. My feelings for Ryan were strong, but my loyalty to my mother was deeply ingrained.

Finally, one night I picked up the phone to tell that Ryan I couldn't talk to him anymore. My heart was racing as the phone rang, and when he answered I felt like my heart sank to my feet. I didn't know what I was doing; I just needed my life to feel easier. This was the first time Ryan even heard about my mother's disapproval. He was shocked and hurt, and it broke my heart to know I had done that to him. I hung up the phone as quickly as I could and cried nonstop for about a week.

My friends saw how down I was after that. After months of talking every day and sharing deep conversations and inside jokes, I felt like I'd lost a best friend. As the holidays approached, I felt lower than ever, and when my best friend Monica asked me what I wanted for Christmas, all I could say, with a mopey face, was "Ryan." A few days later she took me to the mall, and there he was. After plotting with Monica, Ryan had driven to Chicago in a blizzard to see me.

As soon as I saw him there, I knew I wanted and needed to fight for us, but over the next few months, it was Ryan who started to pull away. I had hurt him so badly that he was scared to trust me again. It was more than that, too. He respected my relationship with my mother and didn't want to get between us. We continued to date long distance for several months, but it was always a struggle. We seemed to be in limbo. My mother still disapproved and Ryan was wary of this, which kept our relationship from moving forward. I wasn't interested in dating anyone else, but dating Ryan just seemed too hard.

Finally, after much heartache, I reached a point where I knew I had to let it go. I couldn't keep trying to force things to work out if they weren't meant to, and if Ryan and I were meant to be together, then I knew I wouldn't have to force it. It was so hard to let go, one of the hardest things I'd ever done, especially because Ryan hadn't done anything wrong. But I ultimately decided to give it to God and reminded myself that if He wanted Ryan and me to be together, then it would happen.

Over the next year, I refocused on myself. I worked with a mentor to heal from my relationship with my dad and to create a list of short-term and long-term goals. She helped me get a job teaching with a Good Choices Program in the Chicago public schools. My colleagues were an amazing group of people who taught me to think bigger than I ever had before, to determine what I wanted in life and really grab hold of it. One of the goals on my list was to finish school in another state. Ryan had just moved to Dallas for a new job, and my mentors (who'd always been very much Team Ryan) encouraged me to go there.

I wasn't so sure, but I did find a college in Dallas that had everything I was looking for, so I knew it was worth considering. I kept going back to that "Never chase after a guy" thing, and my mentors would normally never suggest that either. Instead, they encouraged me not to make it my only option or rule it out because of my fears about Ryan and to simply make the best decision for me. I prayed and told God, "I will only apply to the one school in Dallas. If I get accepted and everything works out, then I'll go. If it doesn't work out, I'm not going to force it, and I will take that as a closed door and move on."

To my surprise, everything started falling into place for me in Dallas, and it seemed like things were naturally tying up for me in Chicago. Ryan and I were still in touch as friends, so I broached the topic with him. I was surprised when he didn't exactly encourage it. *Fine,* I thought. *I won't move there for him. I'll do it for me.* Feeling a bit upset about his reaction, I made two decisions: to move to Dallas and to leave Ryan alone. My mother was angry with me for leaving again, but by then I knew I couldn't live my entire life trying to please her. It was time for me to go.

Throughout my entire first semester in Dallas, Ryan and I didn't talk at all. I focused on my work, becoming independent, and living my life to the fullest, and I got to a better place than I'd been in quite a while. During that time, I went on a few dates with other guys, but they could never compare to Ryan. He'd set the bar so high. I heard from Ryan's sister-in-law Julie that Ryan had been asking about me, and after I'd been in Dallas for several months, Ryan texted and asked me to meet him.

"What do you want?" I asked him. I was still angry about how he'd acted when I told him about moving to Dallas, and I was afraid of being hurt again or, even worse, falling back into limbo. Ryan's response was not what I expected. "I want to take you to a basketball game," he told me. "But the one stipulation is that we can't talk about us." As much as I wanted to hash things out, I actually really liked the idea of putting the past aside to see if a friendship was still there. Of course, I still made sure to look really cute!

Sitting next to each other at the game, though we hadn't spoken in months, it just felt right. We started over, and it was fresh and new and yet as familiar as ever. Even better, it felt more mature and stronger. We knew who we were and what we wanted, and this time neither of us would let anything get in our way. While the issues with my mom didn't disappear, the struggle between Ryan and me did. No matter what was going on outside our relationship, from that moment on, it was just Amanda and Ryan again. And it fit.

I wanted to be with Ryan from the moment I met him, but it turns out I wasn't ready for him then. If my mother hadn't objected and we hadn't taken a break, who knows what would have happened? If you'd asked Ryan and me after we'd dated for two months where our relationship was headed, we both would have said, "Married in a year." Looking back now, I know that would have been a huge mistake. At the time, I had no idea what it really meant to be a wife. I'm sure I would have figured it out, but I'm so grateful for the five years I had to grow in wisdom and receive guidance from others.

You have to trust not only that whatever God wants for you will come to fruition but also that it will happen at the right time. You can know exactly where you're going, but if you get there too early, it's not always right. So how do you know when it's time to fight for a relationship and when to call it quits? Maybe you've reached a crossroads. You've met someone you want to be with, but it just isn't working. Being together is too hard, but being apart seems impossible. I can relate to this feeling all too well. And I believe that patience is the connection between pushing forward and moving on. You may think that making any decision at all will bring a feeling of peace, but a rushed decision will often bring only more confusion. If you're conflicted about whether to push through or let go, simply waiting might be the best thing to do. If you're patient and willing to accept any outcome, the best choice will reveal itself in God's timing.

TRUSTING THE PROCESS

Ryan

At the end of that amazing first summer with Amanda, I went back to my college, where I was known both for my leadership activities and as captain of the basketball team. I had a busy social life that included plenty of female friends, but I set the record straight right away. "I'm getting married in May," I told my friends. I started deleting other girls' numbers from my phone. My buddies laughed at me, but I was head over heels for Amanda, and I meant every word.

In retrospect, maybe my friends saw something I didn't, because the truth is that I wasn't ready. I was completely off my game back then. Yes, I loved Amanda from the moment I met her, but I didn't know what it took to be a husband. The way I reacted to our first obstacle just shows how unready I really was. I went numb, and instead of fighting for us, I just filled my life up with enough busyness to distract me from my feelings. I couldn't get Amanda out of my head, but I went back to living my life and being an eligible bachelor.

The fact that Amanda's mom didn't approve of us really threw me. In the past, moms had always loved me. But over time I realized that Amanda's mother actually didn't have an issue with me as a person; she'd never even met me. Her issues with me dating her daughter ran a lot deeper than who I was or even the color of my skin. I thought this would be too difficult to overcome, so I didn't even try. But after that basketball-game date, I knew that Amanda and I should be together, and I began to see her mom's disapproval simply as a hurdle. I knew who God had called me to be, and I had to just continue being that. No one could require any more or less of me.

At that point I was traveling a lot for work, so I visited Amanda's mother whenever I was near Chicago. I even flew up a few extra times just to see her. At first, she wouldn't meet with me. It took me four years and four months to even shake her hand. Over time she slowly opened up, but she still didn't think we were ready to get married. I was already planning the surprise wedding by then and thought I'd made every possible effort. I couldn't keep waiting for her blessing; it was time for Amanda and me to move forward with or without it. So I sent her mom the confidential invitation to the wedding with a note that read, "Amanda and I love you and we want you in our lives. But you need to know three things: I love Jesus Christ. I love your daughter. And we're getting married."

Through all the hurdles that Amanda and I had to overcome, we learned some valuable lessons about how to trust the process and handle obstacles with grace. Here are a few of the most important ones:

Be True to Yourselves

Plenty of well-meaning friends and family members questioned our decisions and wanted us to get married sooner than we did, but this only put pressure on us to act like people we weren't. We had to find the confidence to know when the time was right for us. This meant Amanda had to watch tons of her friends get engaged and married before her, and I'm sure that wasn't easy. But we weren't living their relationships. We were living ours, and we had to do what was right for us. That included winning over Amanda's mother. I really had to ground myself before walking in to see her and tell myself, "Just be you." If she was eventually going to grow fond of me, I wanted her to be fond of the real me.

Evaluate Yourselves

At the end of the day, I'm so glad Amanda's mother kept us apart for so long because it gave me a chance to evaluate what I had to offer Amanda. If you find yourself in a similar situation, use the time to create a system of self-evaluation. One of the ways I did this was to create a checklist of what kind of person I'd want my own daughter to marry and ask myself if I had those qualities. If Amanda and I have a daughter one day, the guy who asks for her hand in marriage better be freaking amazing! With that in mind, ask yourself, "Am I the guy I'd want my own daughter to marry?" If so, you should feel confident stepping into any conversation with disapproving friends or family members, while honoring the perspective other people bring. Although you may feel like you're in love and are the only two people on earth that matter, that's just not true. There were plenty of people in your world and the world of the person you're dating who played a role in both of you becoming who you are. Honor the fact that there are others in your worlds with valuable wisdom, and have faith that if you are good for their son, daughter, or friend, they'll eventually come around.

Work Hard, but Don't Force It to Work

Be honest with yourself. What aspects of your relationship have you been making excuses for? Remember, there's a big difference between working hard on a relationship and forcing it. When you're forcing it, you're jamming a square peg in a round hole and often pretending that everything fits together just fine. Working on a relationship, on the other hand, simply means extending grace to the imperfect person you're dating. Instead of pretending that everything is fine, you're facing your issues head on and accepting the other person's weaknesses. Rather than insisting, "No, no, no, everything is great," you can say, "We're both flawed, and in this moment you wronged me. I'm not going to pretend you didn't, but I am going to forgive you because I value this relationship, and I'm working on it." You should always be willing to put in the work, but you can't *force* yourself to make it work. A marriage is the beginning of something, not the end. Make sure you're going to be ready when you get to the starting line.

One Question to Ask Yourself: What conflict exists in your life that you can use as an opportunity?

One Thing to Remember: Being true to yourself will help you stay the course when faced with challenges in a relationship.

One Thing to Work On: Write down a list of the qualities you'd like the person who marries your son or daughter to have. Ask yourself if you have those qualities.

5

Dating in Community

Where there is no guidance, a people falls, but in an abundance of counselors there is safety.

—Proverbs 11:14, ESV

THE IMPORTANCE OF MENTORS

Amanda

When I was in high school, I went to an assembly thinking it would be a boring waste of time. I got there late and grabbed a seat all the way in the back, and I was shocked when college-aged kids came out on stage and started acting out funny skits and playing videos with current music. It was fun and totally entertaining. At the end, a speaker named Melody LaLuz came up on stage and told her story of being raised in the inner city. She shared her dreams and her goals and told us about her experiences traveling around the world. She was in her midtwenties, single, and truly living life to the fullest. I was in awe of her. Then she told us that she was saving sex for marriage.

I'd always assumed that I would wait until I was married to have sex, but up until that point I hadn't put a lot of thought into it. After hearing Melody that day, I knew for sure that I wanted to wait. I related to her story so much and was completely inspired by her ambition. I'd never met anyone like her, and I wanted to be like her. Meeting Melody was my first taste of what it was like to have someone to look up to, someone who inspired me with her choices and her actions to live my own life in a similar way.

It was after returning from Atlanta and meeting Ryan that I met my first real mentor. Vasti was a friend of my godsister's. Although I hadn't spent a lot of time with her, I'd grown up hearing about her adventures, and I felt like I knew her. When I came back from Atlanta, I ran into Vasti at church, and her reaction to my time in Atlanta was completely different from everyone else's. My friends were all happy that I was back, while Vasti was truly curious about my experiences. She wanted to know what I'd learned and how I'd grown. Because she'd been through something similar, she knew all the right questions to ask. This taught me how important it is to find a mentor who's been where you're going.

It was so refreshing to talk to someone with a different outlook. I felt as if people at home were a little skeptical about me dating someone they didn't know, but when Vasti heard about Ryan, she was the first one to say, "I'm so excited for you." My mom and I still didn't see eye to eye when it came to my relationship with Ryan, so those words from Vasti meant a lot. It felt so good for someone I admired to celebrate Ryan and me instead of being skeptical.

What I really admired about Vasti was her confidence and her conviction to live life to the fullest, even if that meant going against cultural norms. Like me, Vasti grew up in a traditional Puerto Rican family, but she'd left Chicago when she was younger to go to school in Florida. She traveled and met all different kinds of people, and I saw a lot of my own personal ambitions in her.

Vasti called to check up on me every so often, and we grew closer as I began to share more of my experiences with her and ask her for advice. When I talked to my friends about the situation with Ryan, their encouragement and advice was great, but they told me the same things I would have said to them if they were in that situation. We had the exact same perspective, but Vasti was able to offer me a more mature perspective and wider worldview. She never told me what to do, but when I went to her with questions she gave me even better ones to ask myself. Over time, this changed the way I thought and processed things and even how I made decisions.

Vasti made an effort to share special moments with me. I remember feeling so honored when she got engaged and called to tell me. One day, my mom and I got in a huge argument, and I was feeling distraught. I didn't know who else to call, so I called Vasti. She was on her way to her first bridal-dress fitting, but she came to pick me up so I could get out of the house and clear my head. She was waiting in her car, calling me on my cell, but my mom and I had started arguing again, and I didn't hear the phone. When Vasti called me later that night, I told her I felt awful for causing her to miss her appointment. She calmly told me, "Appointments can always be rescheduled. People matter more."

If it weren't for a mentor like Vasti, I don't think Ryan and I would be together—that's how instrumental she was in helping me gain the strength to fight for our relationship. Vasti understood my culture and the difficulties I was facing and gave me the confidence to embrace my own unique path. Every time I felt guilty about going against my mother's wishes, she reminded me of Ryan's character and encouraged me to stay true to myself. Vasti has a lot of respect for my mom and was the last person to suggest that I disrespect her, but she encouraged me to really take time to hear from the Lord and then make my own wise, well-thought-out decisions. Her trust in me inspired me to gain more confidence in myself.

At the time, Vasti was working for the "What's Good" program, a Good Choices Program that served inner city schools. One day I visited her at work, and Vasti introduced me to her team. They were all really cool, down to earth twenty- to thirty-year-olds. After chatting with them for a while, Vasti brought me in to meet her boss, who just happened to be Melody LaLuz, the woman who'd so greatly inspired me when I heard her speak years before!

Melody and I sat in her office and got to know each other a little. Melody was familiar with the leadership program I'd just completed in Atlanta, and we talked about my experiences. Finally, Melody asked me if I was working anywhere. I'd just gotten back from Atlanta and hadn't secured a job yet. Melody told me that she had a feeling I was supposed to be on their team and offered me a job right then and there.

I worked with Melody and her team for a year and learned so much from my married coworkers about what it meant to be a supportive, encouraging wife. One day a few of us were heading out to a school assembly when one of the women, Mari, got a call from her husband.

He was on his way to an interview for his dream job as a chef. I heard Mari encourage him over the phone, and when she hung up she asked if we'd pray with her for her husband. "Of course," the other girls in the car responded. She began to pray out loud for him to find peace and confidence. She prayed that, no matter what the outcome, her husband would know that she loved him and so did God.

I sat behind her in the backseat with a lump in my throat, fighting back tears. It was the first time I had ever heard a wife pray for her husband, and it wrecked me in the best possible way. She and her husband were a team, and it was clear that each was better because of the other. I knew that's what I wanted one day. Ryan and I were still in limbo at the time, but I immediately thought of him and wondered if we could be a good team like they were.

The women I worked with in the Good Choices Program were like my relationship mentors. I learned from them by watching, and with their kind, patient, encouraging words and actions, they taught me how to be half of a thriving couple. When I moved to Dallas not long after that, I was still bitter about the fact that Ryan hadn't encouraged me to move down there. When he called me, I was a little bit rude to him and acted like I was over him. I clearly wasn't. I called Vasti that night and proudly told her, "I straight up told him, 'I'm not one to be messed with, and I do not have time.'" Insert eye roll here! I kind of snickered at the end and waited for her to reply with a "Yeah, you go girl!" But instead of cheering me on, she gave me the tough love that I truly needed to hear. She reminded me that Ryan had always been a gentleman to me, treated me with kindness, and put up with my family chaos. He deserved a better response from me.

This wasn't exactly how I saw that conversation playing out, but I was better for it. Vasti then asked me to write down all my fears about being with Ryan. I did, and I realized that all my fears stemmed either from my family's disapproval or my childhood. Ryan had never actually done anything to hurt me, and I realized that I was really afraid of putting myself out there and being left by a man because that's what I'd seen happen to my mother.

The school I was attending offered counseling, and when I found out it was complimentary, I showed up ready to sort through all of my baggage. In counseling, I began to deal with the past hurts and hang-ups that I'd been carrying around like ugly, broken, cheap suitcases, also known as baggage!

I think everyone could benefit the way I have from having mentors. But—buyer beware—there is such a thing as a bad mentor relationship. It has to be a natural fit and can't be forced. I suggest praying about it and allowing God to bring someone into your life you can aspire to be like. I never expected Melody LaLuz to come back into my life, but when she did, she and her entire team at the Good Choices Program became some of the most powerful mentors I've had in my life. If God brings you someone that you look up to, you don't have to ask that person to be your mentor at that very second. Allow that relationship to happen naturally by asking the person to meet with you and then showing up prepared. Ask about whatever you want to know, leave room for something more, and go from there.

Keep in mind that you should chase your mentor; your mentor shouldn't have to chase you. When you're the one who needs guidance, you have to show up prepared, ask questions, and make yourself available. It's not your mentor's job to follow up, and it definitely is not your mentor's job to fix you. A mentor is there to guide you, not to fill a gaping hole in your life or heal you.

Vasti knew her limits as my mentor, and at one point she encouraged me to talk to my pastor about the issues I was having with my mom. If you need more than a role model, seek a counselor or pastor as well as a mentor so that you can benefit from the wisdom and experience of multiple people who have a variety of tools to help you.

Ryan

When I was in eighth grade, a new girl named Stephanie Syverson came to our school, and we became friends. I started spending time at her house with her parents and her entire family, and I soon found out that her dad just happened to be one of the Illinois state senators. At this time, my dad was sick, and my mom was busy doing everything she could to make ends meet and take care of my brothers and me. They weren't always available to offer the guidance that I needed, and over time the Syversons became my second family. Very often, Mrs. Syverson picked me up from school, brought me to their house, and then drove me home later after dinner. I went on vacations with them and ran errands with them, and most of all I learned from them.

The fact that the Syversons had opened their home to me really left an impression on me. They'd been given so much and were responsible with those blessings. They were amazing stewards of all they'd been given, and I wanted to learn how to do that too. I started asking Senator Syverson questions about life, business, and family, and his answers provided an education that changed my entire world. But even when I wasn't asking questions, I was learning. Their family wasn't perfect, and as I observed how they navigated through their own set of challenges, I absorbed so much wisdom about how a man could lead his family.

Today I can say that Senator Syverson was my first mentor, but I didn't call him that at the time. All I knew then was that if I'd gained so much knowledge and wisdom from one man, then I could probably learn even more if I found multiple people to glean from. When I attended Christian Life High School in Rockford, Illinois, a school connected to a larger church in the area, I started scheduling appointments with the pastors at lunchtime to ask them questions. I wanted to know everything they knew. Some of my friends asked me for advice from time to time, and I wanted to make sure I had something helpful to say to them. First I asked the pastors how they helped the people in their worlds, and then I applied what I learned from them to the people in my small corner of the world. Over time my questions expanded to cover church leadership, parenting, and marriage.

Though the advice those pastors gave me was full of wisdom, it was even more important for me to develop relationships with those mentors and learn from them every day by witnessing how they interacted with their wives, their kids, their coworkers, and their friends. The habit of seeking wisdom from others is what stuck with me, not the advice itself. And that habit has made a profound difference in my life and all my relationships.

From that young age, I found a passion for leadership that lit me up from the inside. I loved bringing insight to a situation and seeing a person go from afraid to free and start doing things he had thought he couldn't do. Then right before I left home for college, I experienced a breakup that really shook me. I arrived at North Central University in Minnesota hurting, missing home, and with a heavy heart.

One day, I walked into the chapel and heard a speaker named Nate Ruch. I was blown away, and it was the first time in ages I'd felt that a pastor was really able to relate to me. I went up to him after he spoke and said, "Thanks for today; that was the first time I really listened in a long time." Nate shook my hand and said, "I feel like we're going to have a strong connection. Talk to my assistant about getting a meeting on my calendar." I immediately went up to his assistant and found out that Nate happened to have an opening later that same day at four o'clock.

When Nate walked into his office at four, there I was. "Wow," he said. "I must have told one hundred other students to make an appointment with me. Most of them never do, but you actually did it." Nate asked me to tell him about myself, and I felt so comfortable with him right away that I shared my whole life story and told him all about my ex-girlfriend.

During that first meeting, he said two things that changed my life. The first was when he asked me to watch a video that really inspired me with its message of forgiveness. When Nate heard how passionate I was about film, he said, "I oversee the video guy for our youth ministry, and he just quit. I've got an office upstairs with all the equipment you need, and if you make our videos for free you can use the equipment whenever you want."

What Nate did that day was give me a sanctuary, a place I could get away and gather myself. That office he gave me is where I started my video business. He also inspired me to forgive my ex for hurting me. I called her later that day and simply said, "I forgive you." I started walking with a bit more pep in my step. It was amazing to feel so different after just thirty minutes with Nate. I knew I needed someone in my life during that season who believed in me more than I believed in myself, so I signed up to be Nate's teaching assistant, just so I could spend more time around him.

When I returned to school for my second year, I was me again. Life had been breathed back into me, and I became captain of the basketball team while taking advantage of Nate's video equipment in a way I hadn't the year before. During that year, Nate called me on stage and gave me his public stamp of approval. My phone has not stopped ringing with opportunities ever since. It's amazing how one relationship has created such an enormous ripple effect in my life. Years later, not only is Nate a cherished mentor, but I feel like I'm a part of his family. I'm close to Nate, his wife, and his kids, and he's helped guide Amanda and me through many of our toughest decisions. In fact, it was Nate who officiated at our wedding.

If you want to be great and have a thriving relationship, you need people who can guide you. But these people aren't likely to seek you out. Instead, you need to find them and prove to them that you're worth investing in. I once got a friend of mine fifteen minutes with Nate. Now, Nate is an extremely busy guy who leads a church, travels around the country, and has a wife and four kids to take care of. Fifteen minutes with him is a big deal. On the day of the meeting, my friend overslept and missed it. I love my friend, but is this the person that a great man and a strong leader is going to want to invest his time and energy in?

I understood from the pastors at my school just how busy people's schedules could be, so I was aware that I wouldn't always be able to get a lunch with someone just because I wanted to learn from them. As soon as I started driving, I began offering to take people to the airport so I could have that time with them. Whenever I met someone who inspired me, I said, "I'd love to ask you a few questions, but I don't need to get on your calendar. Just let me know when you need a ride to the airport." If they had kids, I'd ask when they had a baseball or soccer game coming up, and I'd show up and cheer them on.

These practices not only allowed me to form relationships with multiple mentors, but they also let me observe these men in their natural environments. All my mentors have different relationships with their wives and create unique cultures in their homes, and these personal insights are inspiring. If I'd simply met them in their offices, I would never have seen this side of their lives. When you get close to someone's family, you get a front-row seat to see how they parent, how they spend money, and how they handle conflict. It's much more powerful to watch someone resolve a conflict with his wife than it is to ask him, "How do you resolve conflict with your wife?" Viewing each of these different relationships and putting my own spin on them has taught me what kind of a man, husband, and father I want to be.

By the time I met Amanda, I had so many great people in my life I was confident it was impossible to fail. But without good guidance, we all have the potential to make foolish decisions. Whether we know it or not, we're all being led somewhere by what we observe and what we're told by other people. I can't overstate the importance of having a good guide for the journey.

A mentor is just that—a guide, not a God, a dictator, or a judge. Be careful about who you give authority over your life to. Don't follow any one person blindly; he or she isn't always going to make the right call. There's no way someone looking at your life from the outside can know all the details, so you have to filter a mentor's advice through your own perspective and wisdom.

When I was in college, I was talking to one of my mentors about a girl I was interested in. "I've never seen you like this," he said. "I think you should go see her and tell her that you love her." This was an extremely difficult moment for me. He had such a huge influence in my life, but I didn't agree with him. This girl had me worked up, but I knew deep down that I didn't really love her. I had to muster the maturity to see his advice as insight and perspective rather than a definitive answer, and find the strength to trust my own decision making.

A friend recently broke up with his girlfriend by saying, "Pastor Tim told me that, based on how I was feeling, I should break up with you." Come on, man. You have to own up to your decisions. It's the mentor's job to provide guidance, and it's your job to use that guidance to make your own decisions and stand by them.

Don't be a coward. If you're conflicted about some advice you've gotten from a mentor, pray about it and see what God thinks. Believe it or not, He knows even more than you or your mentor about what's best for you.

FRIENDS WITH BENEFITS

Amanda

Friends are just as important to your life as mentors. Friends often understand you in a different way because they spend more time with you and you're able to be more honest with them. This gives friends more insight into your daily life, and there are certain things that only close friends are able to notice and call out.

Your friends may not be able to give you advice with the same amount of wisdom and knowledge as a mentor, but because you normally see and talk to your friends more frequently than your mentors, they can usually tell sooner when something is wrong or if you start acting differently. When someone gets into a relationship, one thing you hear a lot from their friends is, "She's changed." Of course change can be good. Your friends might notice that you're happier or more content since becoming involved in a relationship, but more often than not, a friend who says, "You've changed," doesn't mean for the better.

Your friends have a perspective on your life that no one else has, so pay attention to what they're telling you. If one friend says you've changed, you can chalk it up to personal opinion, but I'd recommend first examining your own behavior to see if you have, in fact, changed and why. Try taking it to your other friends to get a consensus. Without calling the other friend out, you can say, "A friend told me that I've changed since getting into my new relationship. Do you agree?"

Give your friends permission to keep it real with you so they're more likely to be honest. You don't want all your friends secretly thinking you've changed for the worse while you blindly push forward in a new relationship. Stay humble and take what they have to say seriously. Remember, they can see things from a different perspective than you can.

When I was in college, I had a really great friend, Dave. He'd dated a few girls, but those relationships never worked out. All Dave's friends really liked the girls he dated, and things always seemed to be going great with them until they'd suddenly break up. Our group of friends was starting to wonder if he was a commitment-phobe! One day my friend Jen and I were talking to Dave over dinner, and we jokingly asked him about the commitment issues we'd noticed. Dinner that night ended up lasting for hours as we talked it all through. A week later Dave told us that he'd been thinking a lot about our conversation.

He even talked about it with his mentor, who suggested he go to counseling. There were some issues from his past that Dave had never dealt with and that were connected to his lack of commitment in the present. Dave's mentor probably never would have suggested counseling on his own because he wouldn't have been able to pick up on Dave's commitment issues the way his good friends could.

Mentors and friends can play different roles in your life, but both are incredibly valuable and can make the difference between an average relationship and one that's truly great. I have a handful of friends who were instrumental in my relationship with Ryan when we were dating. My friend Amy has studied psychology and is incredibly wise. She's well traveled and comes from a different culture with a different perspective on relationships.

When I was going through the hard times with my mom, I called Amy and found myself comparing the way Ryan was handling the situation to the way I imagined men in my culture would have handled it.

Part of me expected Ryan to come over and confront my mom the way I'd seen other guys do, but Amy was blunt with me. "Amanda, that's the way you see things," she told me, "but that's not necessarily the way he sees it. Plus, your mom hasn't exactly given him a lot of room to prove himself." That conversation helped me realize that I'd been putting Ryan in the bubble of my culture, but Ryan didn't come from that bubble, and I had to respect that.

Amy was also the first person to tell me that I couldn't compare Ryan to anyone else. "Ryan is Ryan," she told me plainly. "Let him be Ryan, and either accept him for all of him or accept none of it." This was a huge moment for me that helped me see Ryan and the entire situation with my mom in a whole new way. This also shows why it's so important to have friends from different walks of life and different cultures to give you new perspectives on the bubble you've been living in.

More than anything, my friends helped Ryan and me stay together just by supporting us. A lot of my friends were always Team Ryan, and the fact that they accepted him and respected his role in my life meant a lot to me and to him. A few years ago when Ryan and I were on our break, one of my godsisters was dying of cancer. Obviously, it was an extremely difficult time. My friend Monica called Ryan and told him, "I know this may sound weird, but I really think Amanda could use your friendship right now."

Monica knew that despite everything, Ryan was important to me and I needed him then. Ryan called and encouraged me, and it meant the world to me. I know it also meant a lot to him that Monica had thought to call on him. A mentor never would have known how badly I needed Ryan at that moment. It's because Monica and I were so close and spoke almost every day that she knew what his support would mean to me. She wouldn't have done that for just any guy I was interested in. She knew Ryan and found him worthy of my feelings and mature enough to handle such a delicate situation.

Ryan

I believe the person you look up to the most reveals your true capacity, while your friends are mirrors that show you where you're going. When you're in a relationship, it's very difficult to be "inside eyes" and "outside eyes" at the same time. You know what's going on at the core of your relationship, but you can't know what others see when they look at you two. A relationship that only has inside eyes can succeed, but it could be even better if you allow other people to speak into the process and provide perspective.

Do you remember my friend Stacey who spent hundreds of dollars a month on online dating? She recently got married, and the last time I saw her, she asked me, "Ryan, why didn't you shake some sense into me back then?" All I could say in response was, "I did." Stacey nodded. "You're right," she said. "I just wasn't ready to hear it." Are there any valuable messages you're missing out on because you're not ready to hear them yet?

You know you've found a great friend when you don't feel like you have to put a spin on your mistakes or make excuses for the person you're dating. If you're afraid to tell your friends the truth about you and your mate or a decision you're about to make, that's usually a sign that it's not a good fit for you.

My best friend in college once asked me to help him decide whether or not to break up with his girlfriend. He asked, "What do you think of her?" I said, "I think she's horrible—rude, critical, maybe even crazy." I paused and looked my friend in the eye. "But I don't know the girl," I told him. "I only think of her this way because that's how you've portrayed her."

Every time my friend had a fight with this girlfriend, he'd call me and tell me about it, painting himself as a perfect prince and her as purely evil. But I was hearing only one side of the story. For all I knew, she might have been awesome, and he could have been a jerk. "Now tell me about all the good things that you haven't shared," I told him. "I need a full picture of your relationship if I'm going to help you make this decision."

Healthy relationships don't make for sexy conversation. We love to hear about the "juicy" stuff—the drama, screaming fights, broken dishes, and ultimatums—and then we roll our eyes when our other friends report, "Everything's great." When I started dating Amanda, my friends complained that I never talked about her, but I knew that if I told them about our relationship, they'd think it was really boring. I couldn't imagine telling my friends, "We hung out, watched a movie, and then went to a restaurant in our sweatpants," so I found myself embellishing anything I could think of.

My friends responded positively when I talked about Amanda's "feistiness," so I started subconsciously making her seem spicier than she really was. It was more interesting from a storytelling perspective, but I realized that I was painting an inaccurate picture of her. That wasn't fair to Amanda. What if I ended up asking these same friends to help me make a decision about her one day? They'd be basing their advice on inaccurate information.

Whether your relationship is scandalous or completely dull, try to paint an accurate picture of it to your friends.

It's just as important to give your friends the space and permission to be completely honest. Most people lie to you about you. They don't want to hurt you, so they tell you what you want to hear. I realized not too long ago that I hadn't heard my friends say anything negative about me, correct my actions, or call me out on anything in years, so I texted about ten guys and asked for constructive criticism on any area of my life where they thought I had a blind spot. Most of them responded, "Bro, I think you're a good man! Love you." I had to practically beg them to nitpick at my entire life and tell me where I had missed the mark, but when I did they finally ended up sharing some really helpful observations.

Now every few months, I text a couple of friends and ask, "What are my blind spots? What do you see that I don't see?" One time when Amanda and I were dating, my friend Daniel responded by telling me that there were times it seemed I was worried too much about my "brand." He encouraged me to be on the lookout for times when I was concerned about how Amanda was going to make Ryan Leak look. "She's not dating your brand," he told me. "She's a part of your life." He was right on the money. I'll admit that there were times when I thought about how her decisions would make me look, as if now that she was dating me, she represented Ryan & Company. Daniel's perspective was all I needed to shift my mind-set.

There were also moments early in our relationship when I became so busy that my friends had to remind me not to take Amanda for granted. I didn't always realize how much I needed her around, but my friends always knew. This still happens today. Very recently, my father suffered his second stroke. I immediately flew to Atlanta to be with him in the hospital while Amanda stayed at home in Dallas. We didn't know what the next few days would hold, and I didn't want to stress Amanda out with flights and hotels and possibly staying on someone's couch.

At least, that's what I said at the time. The real truth is that I didn't want to stress *myself* out by having to figure those things out for both of us. I knew I'd be fine sleeping on the floor of the hospital if I had to, but if Amanda was there, I'd feel pressured to find us a comfortable place to stay. I'd reverted back to my old ways of being independent and trying to make sure everyone was comfortable and taken care of from my perspective.

The first day I was in Atlanta, my friend Sam came to the hospital and asked me, "Where's Amanda?" I explained that the next three days were pivotal to my father's recovery and she was home waiting to see what happened. He responded, "It sounds like these are three days Amanda needs to be here for." Until he said it, I didn't realize how much I really did need her by my side. After discussing the situation with her, I booked her flight immediately.

What my friends and I have in common isn't the way we look or how we dress or even our taste in music or movies. It's the tough times we've been through that have brought us together. Every relationship can benefit from friends like these. If you don't have good friends, try to be a better friend to others. You can't control how others treat you, but you can control how you treat others. You can't control who shows up for you, but you can certainly choose to show up for others. It doesn't matter if you're popular or a nerd; social status doesn't count during a crisis. Show up and be a friend.

When I was planning the surprise wedding, there were a million times when I wanted to pull the plug on the whole thing. It was too much money, too much stress, just too much everything! I was secretly hoping that someone would slip and tell Amanda because that way I'd get out of it, but I'd still get credit for trying. I told God, "If this isn't supposed to happen, let her find out." We didn't need a rainstorm to cancel it; all we needed was for someone to slip.

But through all the ups and downs, there was one friend or another there to keep my head lifted high and encourage me. I didn't need anyone to discourage me; I had that all sewn up by myself. My friends were in my corner the whole time, constantly reminding me how much Amanda was going to love it and telling me that it would all work out in the end. The people who flew to Miami for the wedding didn't just show up for the event. They were the people who'd shown up and supported Amanda and me during the process of planning the wedding and throughout our entire lives. The success of that event and our whole relationship wouldn't have been possible without that community.

Like it or not, your success is dependent on the community around you and the people in your world. The surprise wedding wasn't just the sum total of Amanda's dream plus Ryan's creativity with the added bonus of great circumstances. The formula would not have been complete without a huge number of great people who were in on it and helped make it happen. If you want to have a great life, a successful career, and an amazing love story, you need more than friends—you need friends with benefits.

One Question to Ask Yourself: Are you missing opportunities to gain an outside perspective on your relationship?

One Thing to Remember: The same relationship can thrive in a good environment and fall apart in a bad environment.

One Thing to Work On: Try to find someone you think has a godly relationship and ask him or her to meet you for coffee once a month.

6

The Other Brother

> [God] made them male and female and said, "Therefore a man shall leave his father and mother and hold fast to his wife, and the two shall become one flesh." So they are no longer two but one flesh. What therefore God has joined together, let not man separate.
>
> —Matthew 19:4–6, ESV

SECOND CHANCES

Ryan

The Christian college I attended brought a "relationship expert" to campus for a week to talk to us about sexual purity. She had plenty of knowledge, and the sessions I attended had solid content. During one of those sessions, I looked at my row of friends sitting next to me. Most of them, I knew, had already drawn a line in the sand regarding their sex lives. Three quarters of them had already had sex, and the remaining quarter had made a strong commitment to stay "pure" until marriage. I sat there listening to this woman make her argument about why staying pure was a good idea and thought to myself, "What if it's too late?"

I also wondered exactly what she meant by "pure." Did she mean that you'd never had an impure thought in your life, that you were simply still a virgin, or some other definition? I knew that all my friends—even the ones who weren't virgins—were good men who were doing their best to follow the Lord's ways. It wasn't fair to slap them with a scarlet letter and say it was too late for them. Maybe you're asking yourself, "Can I still have an amazing love story if _____?" You don't need our help filling in the blank with your past, your complications, your complexities, and the baggage you've packed along the way.

The problem with these discussions about sex is that it's too easy to feel like you're on the outside looking in. I have a friend named Dan who has two younger brothers. He and the youngest brother "did everything right" and are both married with kids, while the middle brother lives with his girlfriend and their son. At a recent family gathering, the middle brother met a bunch of Dan's friends for the first time, and an interesting thing happened. When he introduced himself, people kept saying the same thing over and over as they realized who he was. "Oh," they said with recognition, "You're the other brother."

Unfortunately, many of you reading this probably identify with a label like "the other brother." Maybe when you hear about an amazing love story, you think that sounds perfect for people who've been perfect. But that couldn't be further from the truth. God still has an amazing love story with your name on it, just as He does for Dan's brother.

No matter what you've done in the past, God can always be a part of your future. It's amazing what can make any of us feel like "the other brother," how the rules can put our backs against the ropes in the Christian world because of the things we haven't gotten right the first time. Roughly 80 percent of Christians have had sex before marriage, and I'd say 100 percent of them are trying to hide it. You may have been told that you're damaged goods and that the only way to have an amazing love story is to wait until you're married to have sex. But I don't think it's about where you've been or what you've done. It's about where you're going and the things you do from here on out.

My stance is not against premarital sex; it's against anything that keeps you from your destiny and all that God has called you to do. Most of the time, the person who makes you feel like you're the other brother is you. Don't let your past hinder your future. Use it to propel you into your future. You picked up this book because you want more, you want something great, and the only way to get that is to submit everything you have, including your sexuality, to God.

I was speaking to a group of young adults recently, and a young woman raised her hand at the end and asked me, "Can I still go to heaven if I marry my girlfriend?" Instead of answering right away, I thought for a moment about which people get to go to heaven according to Jesus. There are many verses in the Bible that encourage us to put God in charge of our lives, such as John 12:26, which reads, "If anyone serves Me, him My Father will honor" (NKJV). In Matthew 7:21–23 we learn, "Not everyone who says to Me, 'Lord, Lord,' shall enter the kingdom of heaven, but he who does the will of My Father in heaven. Many will say to me in that day, 'Lord, Lord, have we not prophesied in Your name, and cast out demons in Your name, and done many wonders in

Your name?' And then will I declare to them, 'I never knew you; depart from Me, you who practice lawlessness'" (NKJV).

Jesus is telling us that the people we all assume will be in heaven, miracle workers and company, aren't necessarily shoo-ins. The people who will inherit the kingdom of God are those who've put Jesus in charge and have a relationship with Him.

I looked at this young woman and told her, "Forgiven people and surrendered people—they are who go to heaven. If you put God in charge of your life, your sexuality, and your relationships, then yes, according to Jesus, you'll go to heaven, too." She e-mailed me about a week later saying that she'd surrendered her sexuality and was taking some time to be single and see what God had in store for her. I'll bet it's something really great.

When it comes to sexuality, the Bible gives a lot of great advice for how to avoid sexual immorality from the very beginning, but what is the message for someone who hasn't always made the right choice or followed God's plan? Where does that person fit into this story? I think that many of us confuse what the church may think about us with what God thinks about us, but the God in the Bible is the God of second chances, of redemption and forgiveness. When you believe that something you've done is keeping you away from God, instead of allowing what Jesus has done to bring you closer to God, then you've missed the point of the gospel altogether. If you believe that God's grace doesn't apply to you, then you're missing the greatest thing in a relationship that can make you better, and that's Him.

In the church, the one question that gets asked constantly is, "How far is too far?" Well, from a practical standpoint, I'd say that whatever line you've crossed that has made you ask that question in the first place is probably too far. But I also believe that this question is fundamentally flawed. In God's world, in his kingdom, there is no place you can go that is too far from His grace.

In Luke 15, the prodigal son left his father's home and spent his inheritance on trivial things. The modern-day equivalent might be bar hopping or partying. Then a great famine caused him to starve, and he decided to return to his father, humbly planning out what he would say based on a preconceived notion of his father's response. He thought, "I will set out and go back to my father and say to him: 'Father, I have sinned against heaven and against you. I am no longer worthy to be called your son; make me like one of your hired servants'" (Luke 15:18–19). But when his father saw him coming, he was psyched. He threw his arms around his son and planned a feast to celebrate his return.

The prodigal son judged himself by his actions and felt like an outcast because of his sins. He thought of himself as "the other brother" because he didn't understand the grace and forgiveness his father was capable of. A lot of people who feel like the other brother make the same mistake—they assume they'll be disowned or turned into an outcast for mistakes they've made in the past. Maybe you're still living this lifestyle and wondering what God's message is for you. Well, the message of Luke 15 is the father rushing to you with open arms no matter what you have or haven't done. It's time to stop making assumptions about what God thinks about you and allow Him to give you a second opinion.

In Matthew 9:24 a young girl was pronounced dead until Jesus entered the room and said, "The girl is not dead but asleep." That girl didn't need a miracle; all she needed was a second opinion. Jesus didn't even have to heal her. All he did was give her an accurate picture of who she really was. You may know what the church says about you and what society says about you, but until you get what God thinks about you wrapped around your brain, you'll constantly live beneath your potential. Allow Him to give you that second opinion and surprise you too.

Yes, you should be trying to make wise decisions that honor Christ, but if you've already slipped, there's good news for you. You have something to come back from. The question now is, will you continue down this path or allow yourself to be redeemed? The greatest leaders in history were flawed. The Bible tells us that Jesus's ancestors had the same problems we face today—homosexuality, prostitution, divorce, even baby mama drama—but God sent us Jesus for a reason, and that reason is so those sins can be redeemed. John 4 describes Jesus meeting a woman who'd been divorced five times. Instead of casting her off, He tells her that there is a new life for her, that whoever worships in the spirit and in truth will never be thirsty again.

On our wedding night, I was tremendously blessed to be able to look at Amanda and tell her, "I have been saving my heart, my body, and my soul just for you. There's a piece of me that no one will ever have but you." Whether you are single, dating, or in a relationship, take a moment to think ahead to your own wedding night. What do you want to say when you look at your new bride or groom? No matter what you may have done in the past, you have the opportunity of a lifetime to write that speech today.

If it's too late for you to truthfully say that your spouse is the first person to share this piece of you, that doesn't mean that all is lost. You might have made a million mistakes, but at some point you began to think about the person you wanted to spend the rest of your life with and decided that you wanted to start making better decisions. Before you even met him or her, you chose to prepare your entire life for that person. What a great speech that would make! Despite your past, at some point you drew a line in the sand to make your relationship special. What an amazing love story. You did the best you could, and that's all anyone can ask of you. We want you to make the best speech you can and start preparing now to be the best one you can be.

Take a moment right now to write a speech you'd like to make on your wedding night or a little love note to your future spouse. What do you want to say, and how can you get closer to it? You don't ever have to give it to your mate, but how awesome would it be if you were able to give it and it was honest? What if you were able to say, "Before we ever met, I realized that I no longer wanted to give myself to anyone but you"?

I can't tell you what it's like not to wait for marriage to have sex, but I know what my friends who've experienced it have told me. I was recently hanging out with a friend who was sexually active before he got involved in the church. As we shot hoops I told him, "I honestly don't know what it would be like otherwise." He tucked the ball under his arm and said, "Ryan, I'd give anything not to know."

I wondered about this. Did everyone who was sexually active before getting married feel this way? Another friend, Terrance, was very sexually active before submitting his sexuality to the Lord. I asked him bluntly, "Is what we preach true? Do you look at your past and think, *That was fun,* or do you look at it and think, *Man, I regret it?*" Terrance took about thirty seconds to think about it before saying, "The best way I can describe premarital sex with multiple partners is that it's like spending your whole life trying to put together a puzzle. You've been told what the picture is supposed to look like, but when you look in the box, the pieces in there don't match up. For some reason, you keep trying to put the pieces together, but they never look the way they're supposed to."

Terrance has made a lot of mistakes, but he keeps trying to get it right, and I think that's all you can ask from anybody. He's still working, and his mistakes and regrets have not deterred him from becoming the one God has called him to be. Regardless of what you've done or haven't done, you can still become the best mate possible. No matter where you're coming from, you can still become the best parent possible. It's simply never too late to become the one God intended you to be.

Un-one-ing One

Amanda

When I was growing up, we never talked about sex in my house, and it wasn't until I got to high school that I even started to understand its gravity. Maybe it was just my surroundings, but all of a sudden, it seemed like all of my friends were having sex, and I quickly saw the impact it had on their lives. A few of them would start dating a guy on Monday, say "I love you" by Friday, have sex on Saturday, and then break up the next Monday. After knowing a guy for only a few weeks, they were completely distraught when they broke up.

It puzzled me to see some of my most confident and contented friends get taken over by an attachment to a boy. Sometimes one of my friends would break down crying in the cafeteria or melt down right in the middle of class because she was so overwhelmed by it all. They couldn't let go of relationships and seemed traumatized at the thought of leaving someone, even if he treated her badly. It was such a huge contrast to the home I'd grown up in that wasn't sex driven and had none of this chaos. Sure, any type of breakup is hard, but it didn't take me long to realize that the only thing powerful enough to transform these girls and make them so vulnerable and emotional was sex.

At that point, I hadn't really done any dating myself, but it wasn't always by choice. Until high school, I was super dorky looking, with big hair, one eyebrow, and big round glasses. I'd fallen into the gap of horrible nineties fashion! It wasn't until I entered high school that I learned how to do my hair and tame my brows, and I started to look more like a woman than a young junior high girl. That's when boys started showing an interest in me. By then, I knew that sex held a strong emotional component, and I was determined to wait. If you asked me why I wanted to wait to have sex back then, all my reasons were practical. I didn't want to end up pregnant or with an STD or even allow myself to feel connected and vulnerable with a boy who didn't really know or respect me.

Of course, there were times when I was tempted. There was one guy I met in high school who fascinated me. Devon. He was charming, athletic, funny, and a total rule breaker, and I was "love struck." At the time, I thought he was everything I wanted, but in retrospect I realize that I barely even knew who I was or what I was becoming. What a dork I was to think that I knew what I wanted in a future spouse!

Talk about a moment in life when you wish your adult self could go back in time and give advice to your teenage self. I wish I could tell her, "Hold on, young Amanda! You haven't even scratched the surface of what God has in store for you." Revisiting this time in my life reminds me that God's ways are higher than mine and that His thoughts are greater than my thoughts. He had a bigger and way more wonderful plan for me, and He most definitely has a wonderful plan for you! Thank God I didn't settle for that joker.

But of course I knew none of this at the time. I thought my greatest problem was that Devon wouldn't commit to me and make us "official." We went back and forth for a while, often acting like a dating couple but never with an official title. There were times when he seemed distant and not as engaged as I'd like, and then he'd show some interest, and suddenly I was lying to my mom about where I was going and sneaking out to meet him! He was obviously all wrong for me, which I see so clearly now, but at the time I was fascinated by him. I wish I'd had a mentor like Vasti back then to smack some sense into me and tell me to move on, but thank goodness I did have good friends!

By my junior year of high school, Devon and I were seeing each other pretty regularly, but he was a year older than me and was getting ready to graduate and go away to college. Toward the end of that year, I was with my friends Chloe and Monica at a *quinceanera*. "How lame," I told them with a dramatic sigh. "Now that he finally seems ready to commit, he's leaving!" Chloe shrugged. "Then do something about it," she said. I asked, "Like what?" She looked at me as if I was missing something obvious. "Have you had sex yet?" she asked me.

It had crossed my mind a few times. I knew that he'd been sexually active in the past, and I wasn't naive enough to think that he wouldn't expect that from me if we were in a relationship. I just hadn't put enough thought into it to know what I would do if the moment did arise.

Before I could even answer, my friend Monica stepped in. "What are you talking about?" she yelled, and I looked around, hoping none of the other guests could hear us. "Are you saying that you want my friend to give such an important piece of herself away to someone who won't commit to her and who's *leaving*?"

The passion behind Monica's words really struck me. She'd already had sex, and she knew firsthand how powerful it was. The fact that she felt so strongly that I shouldn't go down the same path meant a lot to me. I already wanted to wait, but at that point it felt like the lights were all turned on and I saw everything for what it was. I ended things with Devon that night, but all of a sudden, he was ready to commit. In his words, "Like, for real this time." But a very small part of me believed that maybe there was someone else out there for me, so I finally let it go.

It was around this time that I started learning about the purpose for sex within marriage and why God created it, and my personal reasons for waiting shifted from practical ones to those that were more spiritual. I now knew that it was pleasing to God for me to save sex for marriage, and I understood that He knew all the practical reasons for waiting and was trying to protect us. Instead of thinking of sex as a bad thing, I saw it as something positive and purposeful within a marriage.

This all came together when I heard Melody LaLuz speak. I already knew that waiting for marriage was right, but what she showed me was that it was possible. She was only a few years older than me, and

I saw the direction her life was going—she was happy and healthy, running her own company, and traveling the world—and I wanted that too. When she spoke about the other direction her life could have gone in, it really resonated with me. There were plenty of girls who'd come up just ahead of me who were already single moms. They spent their days fighting for child support and struggling to make ends meet. They weren't traveling anywhere, and they weren't anyone's boss. I was determined to run in the other direction in Melody's footsteps.

When I met Ryan, I assumed that he wasn't a virgin, and that was okay with me. While it was my personal conviction to remain a virgin and I expected him to share the same boundaries, I didn't assume he'd always held to that standard. It was very early in our relationship, shortly after I returned to Chicago, that we had the "résumé talk." You know the one I mean—you each go through your history of who you've dated, who you've made out with, and who you've had sex with. Since Ryan and I were long distance, we had all our big talks over the phone. I remember how shocked I was during this conversation when Ryan told me that he was a virgin. I was surprised, and definitely impressed. More than anything, it hit me that I wanted to honor his virginity and his reasons for waiting. I took it more seriously than ever for him.

This inspired me to learn even more about sex and all the reasons for waiting when I started working for Melody. Since we couldn't talk about God in the public schools, I did a lot of research and approached it from a scientific angle. What I learned was amazing and convinced me that God designed us to share sex exclusively with our spouses—and created sex to bond us to our spouses! One of the reasons sex is so pleasurable is that it triggers the release of hormones in the brain that act as natural drugs. One of these chemicals, oxytocin, is called the "love hormone" because it literally causes you to feel a strong connection and bond to the other person.

It fascinated me that this was part of God's design for sex because it causes you to bond with your spouse. I felt confident that the purpose of sex was for a husband and wife to share the deepest possible level of connection. Oxytocin is also released during breastfeeding and is one of God's many ways of causing a mother to naturally bond with her child. The problem is that, although God never intended for us to share that bond with just anyone, your body still makes these hormones when you have sex outside of marriage. They cause you to bond with whoever is present at the time, whether that's your girlfriend or the guy you had a one-night stand with. You grow connected to that person, which makes a breakup far more difficult.

The other amazing thing about these natural drugs is that they're addictive. Your brain grows accustomed to these chemicals once it's been exposed to them and starts looking for the next high, just as it does with other addictive drugs. In other words, once you have sex, it becomes harder each time to say no and easier to say yes. This is also because we are all creatures of habit. Everything you do—good or bad—is creating a habit, a pathway to do that same thing again and again. When you make it a habit to give in to physical, sexual urges, it becomes much, much harder to stop.

The bond that's created during sex is referred to in the King James Bible, Matthew 19:5, as "cleave." In marriage a husband and wife cleave, or become one flesh. In college I did a word study about *cleave* to fully understand this scripture and what is truly meant by "one flesh." I discovered that *cleave* is a translation of the Greek verb *proskallao,* which means "to join, cling to, or unite." Think about gluing two things together instead of nailing them to make the bond *unbreakable.* That is why Jesus proclaims in the book of Matthew, "What God has joined together, let not man separate" (Matthew 19:6, NKJV).

What happens when we go against Jesus's word and attempt to separate what has already cleaved together? When you have sex outside marriage, a bond is built through physical action and bonding hormones. You do become one flesh, and tearing that apart afterward is incredibly difficult. You are attempting to break the unbreakable. When I learned this, I immediately thought of my friends in high school and understood all their pain from a new perspective. They were cleaving to the boys that they slept with and then attempting to tear apart what had already become one.

But un-one-ing one is not so easy. The bonds of sex are strong. I'm sure you know someone who has suffered badly after a breakup or even a divorce. I know that my own family was traumatized after my parents had to rip apart what had already been bonded together. When this happens, it's never going to be a clean break. Thank God He can redeem anything, but even He can't completely negate the consequences of going against His wisdom in the first place.

Another interesting thing about the word *cleave* is that Jesus says in Matthew 19:5 that a man shall first leave his mother and father and then cleave to his spouse. Our parents offer us not just a physical covering, but an emotional and spiritual covering, as well. Even if you've been on your own, your parents are considered your protectors until marriage. This is why a man asks permission to marry someone's daughter and why there's that beautiful moment at a wedding when the parents "give away" their daughter.

I cry every time parents walk their daughter down the aisle. When they reach the end of the aisle where the groom is waiting, the minister asks that famous question, "Who gives this woman away to be joined with this man in holy matrimony?" The parents say, "We do," hug their daughter, and gently slip her hand from theirs to his. All of this is symbolic of the parents releasing their covering over their daughter and entrusting their new son-in-law with that mantle.

Our generation has this completely backward. We so rarely abstain from sex until we are emotionally, spiritually, and even financially independent from our parents. It's more likely for young people today to have sex while still living in their parents' homes than to wait until they are fully independent. There's no accountability on either side, and we enter into sex as if it's nothing more than a physical act. Then we suffer needlessly to un-one what we have joined together.

We see this so often in our culture that it's become accepted as normal. Just the other day, Ryan and I were sitting on the couch, flipping through channels until we landed on *Judge Mathis,* a show neither of us had watched since high school. We saw a couple fighting over money during a breakup. The woman came across as so strong and powerful as she stood there demanding money, until the man said that all she was to him was a sex partner. All of a sudden, her entire countenance changed, and she looked completely broken. Ryan and I just looked at each other and said, "That's so sad." This woman gave the most valuable piece of herself to someone who told the world on national TV that to him it meant nothing.

I so badly wanted to tell her that it doesn't have to be this way anymore. I wish this woman could hear the tender counsel of Jesus and make the next man she meets prepare to honor her with a lifetime commitment before she gives that piece of herself to him. So many of us just want to be in love, but it's time to get busy becoming the one with the knowledge that this will be a blessing to you one day.

People are often shocked when they learn that Ryan and I saved sex for marriage. I get that, statistically speaking, we each fit a stereotype of someone who would normally choose a different path. We're both minorities: Ryan was born in East St. Louis, and I was raised in Chicago's inner city. When this topic comes up with other people, their reactions are often comical—they almost fall out of their chairs in shock when we say that we were both virgins on our wedding night.

Once people calm down from their initial reactions, they sometimes shift to the other end of the spectrum and ask, "What's the big deal?" But looking back now, I can say with 100 percent certainty that being married and knowing that I've cleaved only to my husband is the most amazing gift I could have given him—and knowing that Ryan has cleaved only to me is an equally tremendous blessing that I never expected. It's the strongest connection I've ever had to another human being, and it's comforting to know that this is something he's shared only with me and that I've shared only with him.

Something that continues to benefit our marriage is the absence of jealousy or insecurity because we both know that we've never given this piece of ourselves to another person. Waiting for marriage to have sex also taught each of us through Christ how to have power over the desire to have sex whenever we feel like it. My husband is extremely attractive in my eyes, and he was when we were dating, too. The struggle is real! Likewise, putting a ring on your finger doesn't magically make everyone else in the world unattractive. It doesn't even make your spouse the only person you'll ever connect with on an emotional level. But because we trained ourselves to hold back from sexual desires, our skills are strong, and they are able to lift our marriage above temptation each day.

If you haven't had sex yet, I can tell you from experience that it is worth waiting for marriage as God intended. But if you already have, God can redeem that if you submit your sexuality to Him starting now. In God's eyes, it's never too late. If you're conflicted like I was back in high school, remember that His ways are higher than your ways. His thoughts are higher than your thoughts. He has a great plan in store for you, and you owe it to yourself to have faith in Him and find out what it is!

FIGHTING TEMPTATION

Ryan

Whether you've already had premarital sex or not, once you've decided to live a life that's free of sexual immorality, you need to work hard to avoid it. Temptation is everywhere in our culture, and it's not enough to just shrug away from it; you have to actively fight against it. So many of us look at temptation and think, "I'm going to beat you," but if you think you have sin under control, you're wrong. It's so much stronger than you, and the only way to win against temptation is to avoid getting in the ring with it. In our culture we love to flirt with temptation. We put our toe in the water, then get our feet wet, and before we know it, we're up to our eyeballs. Even asking the question, "How far is too far?" implies that you want to toe that line and see how close you can get to the dark side before it's officially called a sin.

In our culture, fleeing from temptation isn't really modeled, but the Bible does not encourage us to flirt with temptation. Instead, 1 Corinthians 6:18 says, "Flee from sexual immorality." I decided a long time ago never to get in the ring with the devil. I put up obstacles and guardrails and make rules for myself that keep temptation away. For one thing, I try not to travel alone, and when I do, I stay at a male friend's house instead of a hotel. This way, I make my mind up before the trip that there will be no opportunity for temptation to sneak up on me at a weak moment. The Enemy knows you and your weaknesses; don't make it easy for him. In James 4:7, the Bible says, "Resist the devil and he will flee from you," and I think the best way to resist him is for you to flee too.

Proverbs 7:4–9 tells us, "Say to wisdom, 'You are my sister,' and call insight your intimate friend, to keep you from the forbidden woman, from the adulteress with her smooth words. For at the window of my house I have looked out through my lattice, and I have seen among the simple, I have perceived among the youths, a young man lacking sense, passing along the street near her corner, taking the road to her house in the twilight, in the evening, at the time of night and darkness" (ESV). I think this is a great illustration of fleeing from temptation. Solomon saw a young man who kept showing up in the street of the adulteress and tells us to call upon our wisdom to keep us away.

Indeed, one of the easiest ways to avoid temptation is to simply avoid showing up. When I was in high school, temptation had an address. I knew that if I went to that one girl's house, bad things were likely to happen, so I stopped showing up. Where does your temptation live? Is it on the Internet, at a bar, or at a certain friend's house? Maybe it's a certain coworker who has you enamored, and every day you find a way to walk by his desk. Maybe it's someone at the gym who has you so intrigued that you've actually memorized her routine and schedule. You know she'll be there at five-thirty when she gets off work, and even though you may not want to date her, you desire for her to simply notice you. Our flirting culture may lead you to get on the machine next to her every day at five-thirty, but a fleeing culture in your life looks like you working out first thing in the morning to avoid temptation instead. Remember, temptation is simply an invitation for your evil desires. It's when you RSVP to that invitation for temptation that sin occurs. It's not a sin to be tempted; it's a sin to give in to that temptation.

When I was in high school I thought my friend Bryant and I were going to be lifelong friends. He'd been dating a girl, Angela, on and off for years, and during that time I'd gotten to be good friends with her, too. At one point, they'd broken up, and Angela convinced me to go on a date with her. I won't lie. I knew it was a bad idea, but she was hot, and I was tempted—not necessarily to have sex with her, but just to be around her. We went out one night and had fun. It was pretty innocent, but things got a bit physical when we cuddled at the end of the night. The next day, I told my friend Bryant what happened, and he was hurt and furious. He never forgave me. I lost a friend that day, and for what, I have no idea. I value friendships so much that this is one of my biggest regrets. I messed up. I shouldn't have let things get physical at all, and if

I could go back in time, I would handle the situation completely differently. No, I haven't always made the best decisions, but I've had a lot of grace in my life. Most of the time, I've been in the right place during my weakest moments and the wrong place in my strongest moments, and that more than anything has saved me from sin.

I think the worst type of sin is a secret sin. When you're alone with your guilt and shame, you become a slave to sin, and that's the scariest place to be. It's when you're alone or isolated from your community that you're at your weakest, and that's when you're most likely to RSVP to temptation. Humans and animals are always their most vulnerable when they are alone. First Peter 5:8 tells us, "Be sober, be vigilant, because your adversary the devil, as a roaring lion, walketh about, seeking whom he may devour" (KJV). In the animal world, lions will never attack wild buffalo in a herd. They always wait for a buffalo to be alone, and then they strike. If that roaring lion can get you alone, it will destroy you, too.

It's an exhausting uphill battle to fight temptation alone. Friends who respect your purpose can help you. But whether or not you know it, your friends are either helping you flee from temptation or they're leading you toward sin. My friends often ask me for advice related to a date. The most common question I get asked about dating is, "What restaurant should I take her to?" Very rarely do I get a call asking, "What can I do to practice my faithfulness?" But of course faithfulness is much more important to a marriage than restaurant selections, and faithfulness can be practiced. If one of my friends asked me that, I'd tell him to pick a commitment, whether it's diet or fitness related or a habit he'd like to make or break—anything that requires discipline for a long time. When you want to quit, don't. That's how you practice faithfulness. True faithfulness is only tested when you want to give up.

I decided long ago that you can't be my bro unless you're going to help me fight temptation. I spoke to a youth group recently, and afterward a young boy asked me, "How do you not let this fame go to your head?" I had rolled in five deep with some of my friends, and before I could even answer, one of them shouted, "Ha! We wouldn't let him. We'd smack him if he got a big head."

Of course, if you're going to fight against temptation, you need to do more than just flee. You also need a weapon against it. I believe the two greatest weapons out there are the Word of God and worship. If you have trouble following the Bible's wisdom about temptation, the very best way to beat temptation is to fall to your knees every morning and ask, "Jesus, what are you calling me to today?" When you're wrapped up in what God has called you to do, there's no room in your life for temptation.

The devil doesn't stand a chance of tempting me when I'm worshipping, when I'm giving glory and honor to Jesus. I have my eyes fixed on where they're supposed to be, so there's no time for me to look to the left or to the right. As you're becoming the one, you have to be honest about your past and serious about your future. Set your mind first thing each day to represent Christ on earth and spread His Word so you can stand strong against temptation. Then the devil has no weapon against you.

One Question to Ask Yourself: What are you flirting with that you should be fleeing from?

One Thing to Remember: The only one who can turn you into "the other brother" is you.

One Thing to Work On: Write down the speech you'd like to make on your wedding night.

7

Leading and Submitting

For the husband is the head of the wife even as Christ
is the head of the church, his body, and is himself its
Savior.

—Ephesians 5:23, ESV

WHAT MAKES A LEADER?

Ryan

We guys are told from a young age that it's our job to be the spiritual leader in our future marriages. This sounds good in theory, but in speaking with young adults around the country, I've found that so many guys are left wondering how to actually do this. The idea of leading the relationship has been passed down through generations and along the way has lost its meaning.

This is also complicated because in Ephesians 5:23, the Bible talks about husbands being the head of their homes and spiritually leading their wives and children, but the Bible doesn't put this expectation on "boyfriends"—or any sort of expectations on boyfriends at all. But if you're looking to create healthy habits for the future, it's a good idea to start leading your relationships now.

So what does it mean to lead the relationship? Well, this goes hand in hand with being intentional. The one thing women want to know at every stage of a relationship is, "Where are we going?" Being intentional means leading the relationship in such a way that you answer this question for the woman without her ever having to ask. If you play games, lead a girl on, or are dishonest about your intentions, you're definitely not acting like a leader. But if you can avoid playing games and ambiguity, you'll be leading in a way that's worth following.

The idea of leadership can be intimidating for guys because they're often afraid of leading and failing. But the one most important thing to remember is that being a leader doesn't always mean having the answers. It's okay to say, "I don't know." Telling a woman, "I don't know where we're going, but I'm thinking about it," doesn't mean that you're failing. Instead, it shows that you're trying. When you're not trying, you're not leading. Trying means acting with integrity and intention, and that's what makes a good leader.

Let's be really honest for a second. A lot of us fail to lead the relationship and be honest with the girls we're dating because we love the idea of remaining available. I wish someone had knocked some sense into me when I was in college. There were girls I took out to dinner and bought gifts for. If you asked them, they'd tell you we were dating, but as far as I was concerned, I was available. I wasn't willing to call it what it was at the time. My friends could still tell me about other available girls or see me with someone else without assuming I was two-timing anyone.

Until you choose to lead the relationship and tell the girl where you stand, you can have this freedom. That is very enticing to a guy, and it was to me, but after a while I realized that I wasn't acting like a leader. A few years later, there was a girl I was hanging out with, and though we weren't dating, I felt that there was some sort of expectation there. I could have easily said nothing and kept hanging out with her, but I wanted to act with intention and lead the friendship, so I told her, "I don't know where this is going, but I don't like being in limbo." She responded by telling me that she'd never seen me "like that." We were free to remain friends without risking anyone's feelings getting hurt, and I thought this was great because then I knew how to act around her. When you're single and you're hanging out with someone of the opposite sex in any context, there's always a question of what's happening between you. The more you can be vocally upfront with the other person and avoid playing games, the better.

But before you can be the leader in any relationship, you have to lead yourself. After all, you can't lead someone to a place you haven't already gone. So the question to ask yourself before attempting to be the spiritual leader in any relationship is, *Where do I want to go?* Your spiritual life can't just mirror the spiritual life of others. Talk to God; ask Him to speak to you. We often hear that Jesus needs to be the center of our relationships, and many of us interpret that to simply mean that both people in the relationship are Christians. But going to church together does not make Jesus the center of your relationship. To actually do that takes an insane amount of intentionality, and it's on you to form your own relationship with the Lord so that you can make it the focal point of your marriage later.

Being a leader means taking steps to be intentional within a relationship. I try to think forward and ask myself, *What can I do for my wife today?* I don't wake up every day feeling madly in love with Amanda. There are plenty of days when I do wake up madly in love with her and other days when there's just so much on my plate that I'm honestly really distracted. But I make a conscious choice to honor the covenant of marriage, and that keeps our love present in our relationship rather than the other way around. In other words, I act with love toward Amanda because I'm committed to her instead of choosing whether to commit to her or not each day based on the way I feel. This sets a loving tone for our marriage.

Here are a few practical steps you can take to be intentional about leading your relationship:

Communicate Your Calendar

I wish someone had told me that one of the most underrated aspects of a relationship is communication about scheduling. The reason this can cause so much tension is because before you were dating, you only had to communicate your schedule with yourself and yourself. You got permission from yourself to go anywhere you wanted. Well, once you're dating and eventually married, you might be surprised by the problems that can be caused by failing to communicate your schedule.

There have been plenty of times when I had plans with my boys for the weekend and forgot to tell Amanda about it. Then on Thursday night she'd ask me, "What are we doing tomorrow night?" It didn't go over too well when I replied, "Nothing." This was my fault for not communicating my plans sooner. We finally learned to set aside time once a week to go over our schedules for the coming week and plan ahead for when we were going to spend time together. This way we knew, for example, that Friday night was date night, Saturday was for hanging out with friends, and we'd go to church together on Sunday. We've recently taken this one step further and started sending each other calendar invites that say things like, "Be at home." We also use this chance to write cute messages to each other in the comments. Most important, it's our way of being intentional about making time for each other and for our relationship.

Guard Date Night

It's extremely important to be intentional about making date nights happen. Come up with a plan and make reservations. Even if you have to cancel later, your plans show that you're prioritizing your time together. Planning ahead makes it that much more likely that the date will actually happen. Speaking from experience, I can tell you that setting this habit early and being relentless about it will make it much easier to keep it going after you're married and have to worry about bedtimes and baby-sitters too!

When you're on your date, if it's at all possible, leave your phone in the car. I know this sounds crazy, but leaving your phone behind sends a strong message that you value your time with the other person. Without the distraction of your phone, you're more likely to actually focus on the person you're with while you're on the date. It kills me when I see couples on a date scrolling through their phones instead of talking to each other! Is that any way to nourish a strong relationship? Of course you'll stop feeling connected if you actually stop connecting with each other. Give yourself a chance to laugh, cry, or just talk to the person you're on a date with without being distracted by your phone. If anyone needs to reach you in case of an emergency, provide the name of the restaurant. This tells the rest of the world to wait in line—tonight is about the two of you. Giving someone your undivided attention is powerful and will go a long way toward protecting what the two of you have.

Hit Pause

Sometimes being intentional with your time just means pausing for self-evaluation. Recently a good friend of mine asked me how I was doing. I immediately started rattling off details about my daily life— "I'm good; I went here; I went there; I met him; I met her; I'm working on this; I'm working on that." My friend stopped me, looked me in the eye, and asked again, "Ryan, how are you *really* doing?" Asking again totally changed the tone of the conversation. I realized that he wasn't looking for a live social-media feed; he actually cared about how I was doing on a much deeper level. This totally rocked my world, and I've been asking people the same question twice ever since.

It's easy to get caught up in the hustle and bustle of a relationship. Things move fast and change every day. While our parents may have held down the same jobs for thirty or forty years and then simply retired, the average length of time we now stay at the same job is only sixteen months. And instead of leaving work behind and heading home at five each day, we take work home with us and live with the constant distractions of e-mails, texts, and social-media updates. If we aren't intentional, it's too easy to lose each other in the chaos. You have to be intentional about taking a moment to really see and hear each other within the daily tour de force of life.

Like I said, I haven't always done a good job at this. Especially when we were dating, I often forgot to clue Amanda in to what was going on with me. Sometimes she had no idea where I was traveling to for work or when I'd be home. Pause and check in with each other before things get this bad. You'd be surprised by what pulling over to the side of the road can do for communication. Some great questions to ask are, "Did I miss anything this week?" and "Do you have anything coming up this week that I can help you with?" And remember, if the other person rattles off an automatic answer, ask the same question twice.

Serve Each Other

Another great way to start leading in a dating relationship is by serving your girlfriend. When you get married, your wife will always have a list of things that she wants you to do around the house or pick up on the way home. If you practice serving her now, you'll find yourself in a place where she doesn't have to ask you for help as frequently. We all naturally want to be served, to have other people do things for us, but making a decision to put yourself aside can create a healthy culture for your relationship. The greatest pictures we have in Scripture of healthy relationships are centered on servanthood. Two people trying to out serve each other rarely split up.

Pray Together

When you start your practice of setting aside time each week to go over your schedule with the person you're dating, make this time an opportunity to create an atmosphere of natural spiritual conversation. Consider saying a prayer over the coming week. Some people think they have to pray together every night, but that's not realistic for everyone. Amanda and I pray together when we feel led to. You decide what works best for you. Sit together and pray that you'll do well at work and that God will bless you with opportunities. Pray for the people you know who are in need, or say a prayer for your relationship. This type of intentionality will help you lead in a way that's worthy of following.

WHAT DOES IT MEAN TO SUBMIT?

Amanda

The biblical teaching that wives should submit to their husbands definitely raises some eyebrows. This idea has become confusing and controversial in our culture, but it's important to remember that it's not just women who are taught to submit. The Bible teaches submission in the context of various relationships. Wives are commanded to submit to husbands (see Ephesians 5:22), children to parents (Ephesians 6:1), and workers to bosses (1 Peter 2:18; Titus 2:9–10). The church is commanded to submit to Christ (Ephesians 5:24), and all Christians are commanded to submit to God (Philippians 2:5–6), government (Romans 13:1–7), elders (1 Peter 5:5), and *one another* (Ephesians 5:21). By submitting to one another, you're essentially forming a team, and you each have your own valuable role to play. I love what Phil Jackson says: "Good teams become great ones when the members trust each other enough to surrender the Me for the We." (Ryan will be so proud of me for quoting a Lakers coach!)

This team-building mentality comes through in Paul's words to the Ephesians almost immediately after he gives wives their instructions. Husbands are commanded to "love your wives, just as Christ loved the church" (Ephesians 5:25). Well, Christ died for the church, so that gives you a pretty good idea of how much husbands are meant to love and honor their wives! Ryan indeed loves me as Christ loved the church. He takes care of me and has my best interests at heart. When your husband honors you this way, submitting to him doesn't feel like going against your own wishes. Instead, it makes me want to serve Ryan and do whatever I can to make his life easier. Because he takes such good care of me, it's truly a pleasure to do whatever I can to help bring him closer to what God has called him to do.

This is a huge reason why you shouldn't settle. If you settle for someone who will not love you as Christ loved the church, it will be that much harder for you to submit to him. Instead of a blessing, it will feel like a chore. When you marry someone, you're saying that you will lay down any of your ways that harm or frustrate him and pick up something new. You're agreeing to honor that person by putting him before anything else in your life and by surrendering the "me" for the "we." Instead of rushing into a marriage with the wrong person and then balking at the idea of submitting to your husband, choose wisely so that submitting to your husband feels like an honor and a joy.

It's important to think about these things early, instead of waiting until you're married to find out what it means for your husband to lead and for you to submit. Start encouraging your guy to lead in the early stages of a relationship. Many women have a natural inclination to get things done, and we can be guilty of bulldozing over a man to make it happen. I know I've done this at times! But there is something awesome about a man who leads without any pressure to lead. Let your guy show his natural leadership by giving him the space to lead. The best way to do this is to pay attention and find out where he thrives and then encourage it with all your might. If your guy is great at mentoring younger guys, encourage him to volunteer with your church's youth group and even take on a leadership role. Or your support can be as simple as going out of your way to thank your guy for remembering to take out the trash! This will give him the confidence to keep pushing forward.

If you have given your man the space to lead, but he hasn't stepped up, it's time to reevaluate things. Maybe he doesn't know how because leading wasn't modeled for him when he was growing up, or perhaps he simply lacks motivation. Encourage him to surround himself with strong leaders so that he can pull from them. Give it time, and if it doesn't change, prayerfully consider if this man is actually God's best for you.

Submitting can be more difficult for some of us than others, based on how we grew up. Recently, we met Kailey at a young-adult group. She told us that the first time she heard she was supposed to submit to a guy her response was "Why?" She'd grown up with a single mom and had only seen strong women leading their families. The fathers in her world weren't leaders; they were absent. This made the idea of submitting to her future husband completely foreign to Kailey, who never had a father figure in her life to submit to or honor. Maybe for you submitting to a guy is difficult because you grew up in an abusive home or because you're dating someone who didn't have good models of leadership in his life.

Kailey needed a new picture of what a healthy marriage looks like to see how it works when a husband is a strong leader and his family wants to submit to and honor his leadership. Luckily, Kailey's pastors, who were husband and wife, opened their home to her and some other girls who'd grown up in similar circumstances. Kailey told us that she'd never seen a black man who was so involved and present with his family. I can relate to this since I didn't see a lot of that growing up in my culture, either. In her pastors' home, she saw a man who led his family with strength and love, and this has completely changed what Kailey is looking for. Now that she knows this type of marriage exists, she is waiting to meet the loving, caring, present man who will be the one for her.

LEADING THE WAY FORWARD

Ryan

Most relationships naturally reach a point where it's time for the two of you to either get serious about marriage or go your separate ways. Since the man is the one leading the relationship and the one who normally proposes, relationships can get stuck when a guy isn't certain that he's ready to commit to this girl but doesn't want to end things with her either.

If this happens, it's time to get really honest with yourself about what's stopping you from moving forward. Is it her? Is it you? Or are you just not ready yet?

If you're not sure about this girl, do your best to define your concerns so you're aware of what's causing your hesitation. In relationships we so often sweep concerns under the rug and then only lift the rug when we're in the middle of a fight, but this isn't grace or true forgiveness, which are both crucial in a relationship. If I could go back in time, one thing I'd like to do better is look at the things under the rug when things were going well. Don't wait until things get bad to see what's under there! It's when things are running smoothly that you can see those concerns through an accurate lens instead of letting anger, fear, or resentment blow them out of proportion.

For an even clearer perspective, try writing down your concerns and running them by a mentor. A guy who heard me speak recently contacted me afterward with what he called a relationship crisis. He told me that his relationship with his girlfriend was falling apart because she was texting with her ex-boyfriend. It wasn't until later in the conversation that he told me he was still married. He was separated from his wife, and his girlfriend didn't know they weren't yet divorced. This guy thought his biggest problem was a text message when he was still secretly married to someone else.

What he needed was a mentor or friends who could give him some perspective about what's actually a big problem in a relationship and what's a small problem. He didn't know any better, and I honestly don't fault him for that. But if you want a thriving relationship, I encourage you to make an effort to know better. Don't feel foolish approaching someone you trust and saying, "On a scale of 1 to 10, how concerned should I be about this?"

You have to ask yourself if the reasons you're not willing to move forward are because of her perceived weaknesses or your own. Nine times out of ten, a guy's lack of commitment points to his own weaknesses, not hers. So many guys think they're "not ready" for a serious relationship, but to me that's the beauty of commitment. It pulls things out of you that you didn't know were there. The goal is not to be ready but to be *responsible.* You can't control the future, but you can control what you do today. Be a great steward of everything you have today, and the rest will take care of itself. If you say you're not ready to take the next step in a relationship but play video games for three hours a night, then your issue isn't whether or not you're ready. Your issue is that you don't want to be ready.

A lot of young men ask me, "How will I know when I'm ready?" I tell them that when you can look at your money, your possessions, and even your career, and you're at a place where you're able to put all of them on the table for the person you're dating, you're ready for marriage. Of course, you want to be with someone who will never make you give up those things to be with them, but it's a sign that you're ready when you're willing to give them up. We all have the potential to let our careers get in the way of our relationships or prioritize other things over our spouses. It's okay if you're not there yet. You can start slowly by letting go one step at a time, consciously allowing moments to happen when you choose the other person over yourself. If you keep on having those moments, they'll stack up until you find that you're ready.

For me, it was when I was okay with never going to another Lakers game or ever traveling again, if that's what it took to be with Amanda, that I knew I was ready. Sure, I was living the dream flying around and watching my Lakers play, but it was more important for me to come back home to Amanda. That's when I realized that she was the most important thing in my life. It took us a long time to get there, but it was worth it. And I was excited to lead our way forward together as one.

DETERMINE THE RELATIONSHIP

Amanda

With the man leading the relationship, a lot of tension can arise when he's not moving toward an engagement or marriage as quickly as his girl would like. This often becomes a problem when the relationship didn't have a lot of intentionality in the first place and the man didn't take on a strong leadership role from the start. You both should be aware that the girl in the relationship is almost always going to start thinking about marriage long before the guy. That's okay! As women, we're generally wired to be this way. (Of course, there are some exceptions.)

If you've been dating for a while and haven't discussed marriage yet, be careful because you run a high risk of landing smack-dab in the middle of a DTR—a Determine the Relationship talk. It helps to be prepared for a DTR, so recognize that it's about to happen to you. Guys, the main sign that you're about to have a DTR is hearing your girl say, "Baby, we need to talk." Those are words no guy wants to hear!

Guys are less likely to instigate DTRs when they're already in a relationship and usually reserve them for when they want to take a friendship with a girl to the next level. Ladies, if one of your guy friends starts acting funny, make sure to be on the lookout for terms like "I've been thinking" and any use of the word *us*. These are huge giveaways that a DTR is coming.

Most guys dread DTRs, but remember that they are preventable. The best way to avoid a DTR is to beat the girl to the punch. If you don't begin the DTR, eventually she will. Think about what Ryan said earlier about leading. A good leader will let his girlfriend know where things are going. It's always good to talk honestly about where you are right now and where you see things going, even if you're not sure. Too often, girls are left wondering if the guy is thinking about marriage or if he's even serious about her.

Ladies, if you find yourself getting antsy about where your relationship is going, you have every right to find out. That doesn't mean you should sit your guy down and demand answers. Instead, tell him how happy you are in the relationship and that you do see marriage in your future. That's it! This way, he'll know what you want but won't feel the pressure to figure it out right away. It will give him the confidence to start thinking about marriage on his own terms.

If you've had this conversation with your guy a few times and nothing's happening, it's time for a more serious DTR. This should be a very practical conversation, not an emotional one. Calmly tell him, "I'd like to get married eventually, and if that's not where you are and don't see that for us in the future, I can understand that. I would never want to force it, so I wanted to hear from you before I decided to move on." When you approach the subject like this, it's amazing how quickly things can change. Saying what's on your mind plainly forces the guy to look deep within himself to find the real reason he may be stalling so he can either let you move on or reevaluate. The former is a harder pill to swallow, but at least you'll have clarity. It's always better to know if a relationship is ending than to remain in a relationship that's heading nowhere.

A pastor once told me that when he was younger he was living with his fiancée and two young daughters. He admitted that he was a horrible partner and took his fiancée for granted. In his words, he "treated her like crap," and was the furthest thing from a leader in his home. One day when he and his fiancée were lying in bed, she told him in a completely calm voice, "I'm leaving, and I'm taking the girls. Nothing about your relationship with them will change, and I will do my best to make sure you see them as often as you want. I will always love and care about you. Don't worry; we'll all be fine. You'll go on to do great things, and so will I."

The pastor told me that it wasn't so much what she said that got to him, but the way she said it. They'd fought plenty of times before about their relationship issues. They'd yelled and screamed and insulted each other, but this time was different. He knew that something had changed, and he said that, for the first time in his life, he wept. It hit him how much she had meant to him and how royally he had let her down as a leader in his home. He went out for a long drive that night and prayed to God that He would restore what he had broken. The next morning he went home and asked his fiancée if she would forgive him and allow him to pursue her all over again, this time allowing God to direct him. She gave him one chance, and that chance has lasted for more than twenty years of marriage!

Ladies, if you're dating a guy who isn't thinking about the future, rather than putting pressure on the guy, get the ball in your court. Submitting does not mean waiting forever if he's not leading you in a way or at a speed you're comfortable with. Tell him where you draw the line, but you have to be willing to deal with the fallout. You don't know how he'll respond, so be open to a conversation. He may say that he really does want to marry you but doesn't feel ready financially. Waiting to be financially stable is a perfectly good reason to delay an engagement. If that's the case, be understanding and supportive, but set concrete goals in order to move forward. Ask him where he would need to be in order for it to happen, and then if he doesn't deliver against those goals, you'll have your answer.

You may not like it, but when the signs are clear, it's your turn to act. You don't want to be married to someone who's not sure he wants to commit to you. Neither do you want to walk away from someone who's moving in what he feels is God's timing just because it's not fast enough for you. Prayerfully consider both options so you're not following him around in circles or trying to drag him to the finish line.

Guys, it's important to know there may be a period of time when your girl is thinking about marriage and you may not be. This doesn't have to become a source of conflict if you're aware of it and lead intentionally. One thing I really appreciated about Ryan when we were dating is that he was always really honest about where he was, even when he wasn't ready for marriage. He once sent me a card that said, "I may not be where you are, but I'm still here." That could have been a hard truth for another woman, but I appreciated his honesty and intentionality.

You don't have to be on the exact same timeline in order for you to lead your girl and reassure her. If you are affirming throughout the relationship, where the relationship is going won't be such a sticky and uncomfortable topic; the conversation will just flow naturally. Girls tend to freak out when they're in a relationship with someone they see a future with but who hasn't vocalized his intentions. If you reassure her before she starts to worry, she probably never will.

All right ladies, you may want to skip this paragraph because you may not like what I have to say, but I promise that I'm saying it 100 percent with you in mind. Fellas! Because the guy is usually the one to propose, I think that if you have some major doubts about the relationship and don't see a future with this person, and you've gotten feedback from trusted sources, and you know the girl you're dating is thinking about marriage, you should end the relationship. The proposal will set everything in motion, so the relationship is essentially waiting on you. If you're not ready or unsure, you need to think about letting the relationship go.

I have a friend whose boyfriend broke up with her not too long ago. At first she was crushed because she'd seen a future with him, but after a while she got her priorities in order and realized that she'd been putting a lot of things in her life on hold while she waited for a proposal. After they broke up, she quit the job that was making her unhappy and started to pursue her real passions. When I saw her recently she was more content and full of joy than ever.

Guys, don't wait for a girl to give you an ultimatum—put an ultimatum on yourself. And girls, don't put the rest of your life on hold while you sit there waiting for a ring! Whether you're single, dating, or already sporting something sparkly, making the most of this season will always help you transition effortlessly into the next one.

One Question to Ask Yourself: What can you do today to prepare to lead your wife or submit to your husband?

One Thing to Remember: Two people trying to out-serve each other rarely split up.

One Thing to Work On: Practice servanthood by finding someone in your community you can serve.

8

Setting Expectations

Love never gives up. Love cares more for others than for self. Love doesn't want what it doesn't have. Love doesn't strut, Doesn't have a swelled head, Doesn't force itself on others, Isn't always "me first," Doesn't fly off the handle, Doesn't keep score of the sins of others, Doesn't revel when others grovel, Takes pleasure in the flowering of truth, Puts up with anything, Trusts God always, Always looks for the best, Never looks back, But keeps going to the end.

—1 Corinthians 13:4–7, MSG

WHAT IS LOVE?

Ryan

People say "I love you" all the time, but few of us take the time to really think about what these words mean. What is love? The Bible speaks of three types of love: *phileo* love, *eros* love, and *agape* love. Phileo love is a brotherly, affectionate love you might have for a close friend or family member; eros love is a passionate, romantic love; and agape love is a higher, more powerful love that is sacrificial in nature. Agape love isn't about feelings at all; it's an act of will. This is the love that God has for His people and the reason He sacrificed His Son for our sins.

My dad has shown me agape love since I was born. My dad is old school. He was fifty years old when I was born, and he always seemed like he was from a completely different time, which I guess he was. The man never owned a pair of jeans and seemed to have the most amazing spiritual slogans in his back pocket like, "In 2007, we're all going to heaven." But there was a lot more to my dad than that, and I loved it when I got to see him in his element—speaking at church, leading people, and inspiring them. We're very different people, but one thing we have in common is our mutual love of McDonald's. When I was growing up, every time our family was trying to decide where to eat, my dad would say, "You know what I could eat? I could eat some Mickey D's Steakhouse." That's what he calls it to this day.

Whenever my dad traveled to speak in a different town, I went with him, and we made a road trip out of it. And when he was done speaking, he always bought me a Happy Meal from Mickey D's Steakhouse. I loved traveling with my dad, just sitting in the car with him. We didn't have to talk; we were just cruising, and those are some of my happiest memories of my childhood.

I was in the fifth grade when I woke up one morning knowing that something was wrong. My parents must have faced their fair share of struggles as I was growing up, but they did an amazing job of protecting me from them. This time, before I even got out of bed, I knew something bad had happened. The house was dark and quiet. I went downstairs and saw my mom and brothers in the living room, huddled together in prayer. Flashing lights outside the window caught my eye, and I saw an ambulance backing out of our driveway. I knew right away that my dad was in the back of that ambulance, and I told myself that at least that meant he was alive. My mom quickly pulled me to her and said, "Ryan, your father has had a stroke." At the time, I had no idea what a stroke was or the full gravity of the situation. But somewhere in the back of my mind, I knew that everything had changed and I would have to grow up a lot faster than I wanted to.

It was a miracle that my dad recovered from his stroke. The doctors said he'd never walk or talk again, but fifty-two days later, he walked out of the hospital chatting up a storm. Although he was very much alive, his mind and body weren't as strong as they were before the stroke. He could no longer drive, work, or physically do many of the things he was accustomed to doing, but he was just as positive as ever and determined to be the same man and father he'd always been.

Because he couldn't drive, my dad had to walk miles to a bus stop just to get to my basketball games. He did this successfully countless times, but there were also times when he promised he'd be there and miscalculated, missed the bus, and failed to show up. I didn't blame him for this. I knew he was doing everything in his power to be there for me, and I appreciated it, but it was still disappointing when he didn't show. No matter how proud he said he was of me or how many times he told me he loved me, it meant so much more to me when he actually made it and could physically show his support.

My dad is a dreamer just like me, and he gave me everything I needed to fulfill my dreams. As I got older, I realized that I was standing on his shoulders, and I promised myself that instead of relying on words to tell people how I felt, I would be there for them in all the ways he couldn't be anymore. I decided that it was important to show agape love: Christ's love in action. My dad first showed me what this type of love looked like, and I wanted to carry on his work. I became a doer instead of a talker, and actions became far more important to me than words.

In high school I found ways to show my friends what they meant to me instead of relying on words. I started trying to come up with thoughtful gifts to show them how I felt. I found the kid who was sitting alone in the cafeteria and bought him a sandwich. Over time, giving gifts became my love language, and I never told people I loved them until I knew I'd already backed it up with actions.

LOVE VERSUS ROMANCE

Neither agape love nor phileo love has much in common with the eros or romantic love we see on TV and movie screens, which is all about emotions and how you feel right in the moment. Hollywood's finest writers and directors do a great job of creating pictures of love that capture our hearts and imaginations for an hour or two. We then leave the theater believing we know what love looks like. Love is sexy. Love is full of surprises and witty banter at happy hour. Love writes a song. Love brings flowers by your job. Love puts butterflies in your stomach. Love buys you courtside seats. (Go Lakers!) Love has your same sense of humor. Love catches the flight at the last minute. Love tells you exactly what you want to hear, just when you want to hear it. Love notices when your hair looks different and when you got a new purse. Love gets engaged and married on the same day.

That's all cute and amazing, but that's not love—that's romance. And while Amanda and I strongly believe in romance within a relationship, we can't confuse that one element of a relationship with the sum total of an accepting, sacrificial, willful agape love. In 1 Corinthians 13, we learn that love is patient and waits when you want to leave. Love is kind and keeps no record of wrongdoing, even when it's easier to keep score and hold a grudge. Love tells the truth always, even if it's hard to say and even harder to hear. Most important, love trusts God. It's not about what I want, what Amanda wants, or what you want. Love means accepting and embracing God's best for you.

Agape love may not look as sexy as what we normally see on the screen, but when lived out it's far more powerful than a tweetable moment that impresses people. Tomorrow everyone's news feed will refresh, and that moment will be gone. My latest Facebook post might have gotten two hundred Likes, but no one will even remember it tomorrow. It's no wonder the brother of Jesus said in James 4:14, "What is your life? You are a mist that appears for a little while and then vanishes."

Romantic moments are a part of that mist. They're the cherry on top of the cake, but they're not the cake itself. Too many of us think that we feel love based on what it looks like on the screen. Whenever we find ourselves in a moment with a potential mate that reminds us of what we've seen on the screen, we assume that we're "in love." The question I always ask my friends when they tell me they're in love is, "Why do you love him or her?" When the answer is because of a temporary feeling or even attributes that are temporary—like his or her looks, job, or money—I know that really isn't love. My friends may have strong feelings for the other person, but that person's looks may change drastically in a decade, people lose their jobs all the time, and money can be gone in an instant. It's a part of the mist that will be gone with our next breath.

I felt that romantic, chick-flick version of love for Amanda on day one, but it took five years for me to be ready to sign up for life with her. And until I was, I never told her, "I love you." That's right—love at first sight and five years of on-and-off dating, and not once did I tell her I loved her. When some people hear this, they assume I was holding out on her, but God's love, described in John 3:16, includes *laying down your life.* John 3:16 depicts a God who was willing to sacrifice Himself for the people He loved, and when I finally said, "I love you," to Amanda, I was saying, "I'll die for you." Nothing more and nothing less.

ROMANCE VERSUS COVENANT

Romance is awesome and should exist in your relationship daily, but it shouldn't be the thing you aim for or serve as a measurement for how you are doing. Two kids, a new career, and a decade later, you won't have time to go on nearly as many dates as you did when you were just boyfriend and girlfriend. How are you going to measure the quality of your relationship then? Our wedding story is so fun for us to tell people when we meet them for the first time, but that's all it is—our wedding story. It's not our marriage story, and there are many chapters to be written in our love story that don't involve viral YouTube documentaries.

If you allow the popular picture of romance to set your goal for falling in love, does that mean you have the freedom to walk away when you fall out of love? When we're just not feeling it anymore, can we simply pick someone else to try to fall in love with? Are you going to honor the other person merely based on how you feel that day?

I don't think God intended for us to marry someone based purely on romantic feelings. Instead, God created covenant so that a husband and wife would *choose* to love each other every day, even when they don't feel like it or the other person doesn't deserve it.

I think the greatest picture of love in the Bible is the story of Hosea and Gomer. God tells the prophet Hosea to marry Gomer, who was basically a prostitute. Take a moment to think about that. Hosea was a prophet, a modern day megachurch superstar pastor marrying a harlot. Imagine what Twitter would do with that today! At one point, Hosea has to go to the brothel and buy his own wife back. The number one reason God had Hosea do this was to show His people what His love for them truly looked like.

There's a point in the Hosea story when Gomer is putting on her pearls and perfume to go meet her lovers. Can you imagine a husband standing in the doorway of the bathroom, watching his wife get ready for other men? And when she goes with those other men and they abuse her, Hosea goes and gets Gomer and brings her home anyway. This is the love God shows us, and this is what it should mean when we say, "I love you." I love you despite your shortcomings. I love you *regardless* of my feelings. I love you enough to *buy you back,* and when times get rough and your mate wrongs you, love buys you back. Love forgives the other person when you'd rather hold on to bitterness. Of course, this type of great sacrificial love can only work with two things—God's help every day and a well-chosen partner.

This idea of covenant has lost its appeal in our culture that holds the drama of romance in higher esteem than love, but I think we all need covenant more than we realize. Amanda and I have a great friend named Liz who is a triathlete superfriend, a superwife, and an all around amazing person. While we were writing this book, Liz got pregnant. She and her husband, Chris, were very excited because they'd lost a baby during a previous pregnancy. A few months into this pregnancy, they went for a regular checkup and got some devastating news. Liz had a cancerous tumor on her cervix. The doctors wanted to begin treatments right away, but they couldn't while she was pregnant. They said there was very little chance of her being able to carry the baby to term or the baby even surviving, so they recommended that she abort the baby and begin chemo to try to save herself.

Liz and Chris were obviously devastated, and they faced an incredibly difficult decision. To make things worse, they could not find a doctor who'd support their decision to continue the pregnancy. After months of battling doctors and hospitals, Liz went into early labor and gave birth to a beautiful baby girl at twenty-nine weeks. She'll be on a breathing tube until her lungs develop, but otherwise she's perfectly healthy. And now Liz can start cancer treatments earlier than planned.

Take a moment to think about who you'd want to face this type of heavy decision with. Trust me, throughout all this the last thing on Liz's mind was whether or not Chris remembered her favorite type of flower. It was far more important that he was there, fighting right alongside her. She'll be the first to tell you there's no trip to Paris that could compare with the type of comfort that only comes with real covenant.

You don't know what lies ahead, but life itself pretty much guarantees that there will be storms. Tragedy is on the horizon for all of us. None of us are exempt, and it's in those moments of despair that we finally learn that covenant isn't so bad after all. But you don't have to wait for a tragedy to wake you up and show you what's important. You can act preventatively and honor covenant now, before you need it, by choosing carefully the person you want to brave the storm with. It's easy to get an emotional feeling after a great date when you're all dressed up and life feels effortless, but a storm is coming. Who do you want to face it with?

We're all going to face storms, and we're all going to face moments when we're the ones who need to be shown God's grace. It's easy to overlook the importance of covenant when you haven't been tested and you feel like you're the Hosea, the good guy, in your love story. But when you're the Gomer and you have someone who's going to stick by you for life, despite what you may have done or said in the past, you'll be grateful for covenant. What most people don't realize when they're single is that every one of us is the Gomer at some point in our lives, and we all need a Hosea. We're all flawed individuals, and when left to define what love is by ourselves, we'll fall in love and fall right back out of it. God's love as beautifully depicted in the book of Hosea is a story about choice, about an agape act of will. You don't slip and fall into covenant, and you won't accidentally fall into an amazing love story, either.

THREE LITTLE WORDS

Amanda

As soon as Ryan and I got back from our honeymoon, Jeff, the videographer who filmed our wedding, came to Dallas to interview Ryan and me for "The Surprise Wedding" documentary. Everything was still so fresh in my mind. I'd just learned about all the planning that had gone into the wedding, and I hadn't fully processed it yet. Jeff asked Ryan about waiting to say "I love you" until he proposed, and I thought, *We should probably mention that I never said it until then either.* But the opportunity never came up, so I just brushed it off, thinking it would mostly be our friends and family who'd end up watching the video anyway, and they'd understand.

A few months later Ryan and I filmed an interview with *Good Morning America* and then went our separate ways. Ryan flew to New York for work, and I headed to Chicago to visit my family. While I was in Chicago, the number of views of the video really started picking up, and so did the comments. I remember sitting in my mom's apartment reading what people were saying about us. One woman asked, "What kind of guy doesn't say I love you for five years?" I was tempted to jump in and defend Ryan until I saw another comment: "Don't you think a guy who did this would reassure her in another way?" I laughed as viewers argued back and forth about our very personal relationship, which was suddenly very public.

All those people who were commenting seemed focused on one thing—the fact that Ryan waited five years to say "I love you." People struggled with watching something so romantic and then hearing something that didn't fit with their perception of romance. In romantic comedies, the characters often jump to say, "I love you" after a great first date or a nice kiss. Most of the time, the main characters say those words within the first thirty minutes of the movie. They say them be-cause the moment has been set up for the words—the music is swelling, the sun is setting, emotions are peaking, and the entire script has been written around this moment.

"The Surprise Wedding" video felt very romantic in similar ways. Ryan and I were smiling and happy and looking and feeling our best. And then Ryan states that he's never said, "I love you." For many viewers, that did not line up. Some of them even complained about the fact that Ryan said the words for the first time in the car on the way to the place he'd planned the proposal. They're used to seeing people say, "I love you," for the first time during big, grand moments instead of while making a left. Sorry for the letdown, but that moment wasn't meant to impress others. It was real and raw, and that's life. To me, Ryan's "I love you" was more romantic and meaningful than any movie moment.

I never thought I'd end up waiting until my wedding day to say, "I love you," but I did know that when I said those words, I wanted it to be special. What does *I love you* mean when you say it to the second or third or fourth person you've dated? Does it mean "I like you" or "I really like you" or "I like what I know about you so far"? I knew that when I said, "I love you," I wanted it to mean, "I find you worthy of committing my life to," and I hoped that when a man said the words back to me, he meant he found me worthy too.

DEFINING LOVE

By the time I got to college in Dallas, I was a couple of years older than the other girls in my dorm. They'd often come into my room after a date and talk to me about it. Sometimes I offered advice, and other times I just listened. I remember one girl telling me, "It just felt right, like we were in a movie, so I told him I loved him!" She seemed so happy and excited, but I wondered exactly what she thought she was saying to this guy when she said, "I love you," and what he thought she meant by it. If she was inspired to say it because it felt like they were in a movie, would she no longer love him during a mundane moment, when they're stuck in traffic and he has caused her to be late for an important event, or she and her boyfriend are shopping for groceries and grossed out by each other's choices? Is love really dependent on things like location and scenery?

When you're in a relationship, what do you gain by rushing those words out? Not much more than a sweet moment, but there are plenty of other ways to achieve that—romantic moments shouldn't be hard to come by when you're dating someone you believe you love. On the flip side, rushing to say, "I love you" before you fully understand what it means can cause a lot of problems. It only takes a second to say, "I love you," but those words hold a lot of weight. And because agape love hasn't been defined for our generation, everyone has his or her own perception of what it means. If a girl tells a guy, "I love you," meaning "I want to be with you forever," and the guy interprets it to mean "I really like you," they're going to have very different expectations for their relationship.

One of the girls I mentor was in a relationship that started off great. She and the guy she was dating said they loved each other and were having fun. And then things got bad. He had some anger issues and started having blowups. They broke up, but afterward she really struggled with her decision. She kept looking back at the good times they'd had together and wondering if she'd made a mistake. Months later I was talking to her on the phone about it, and she kept saying, "But he loves me!" Sweet girl. I had to tell her the facts this time. "That's not love." I repeated what the Bible says about love (which you can find at the beginning of this chapter) and asked her, "Does any of this sound familiar to you?" Finally, she got it, as if a thousand bricks had fallen on top of her head, all marked "Truth." She felt the full gravity of a fraudulent "I love you."

If you rush to say, "I love you" before you fully know a person, will you be able to take those words back after you get to know this person better and discover something that is truly unlovable? I'm definitely not saying that you should say those words only after getting engaged or married. You decide for yourself. But I do think that once you're in a relationship, you should spend some time together defining what those three words mean for you. Then when you do get to the point when you can say them, you'll both have the same understanding. Protect these words by defining them together.

Even in the very beginning when Ryan and I were dating, some could have described the way I felt about him as love. I enjoyed spending time with him, I was super attracted to him, and I thought about him night and day, but the affection I saw between couples who had been married for decades seemed to go so much deeper than that. One of my professors and his wife were in their sixties and were madly in love with each other. It was obvious to everyone from the way they looked at each other and talked about each other with such reverence. My professor went to the store every so often and bought his wife a gift to keep in the trunk of his car. He drove an old beater with the backseat piled high with books and the trunk filled with jewelry, perfume, and purses for his wife. Whenever his wife was having a bad day or a rough week, he'd go digging through the trunk for the perfect gift to cheer her up.

One day I was sitting in class waiting for him to begin his lecture when his wife walked in and surprised him. She turned to the students and said, "Class is dismissed for today. I'm taking my husband on a date." She already had permission from the dean to cancel class that day. They looked each other in the eye with an expression of pure love, and seeing this was a greater lesson than anything he could have taught us. They shared a quiet, confident love that was different from the butterflies and excitement that our generation describes as love. Thirty, forty, fifty years of sacrifice, commitment, illness, bankruptcy, and total acceptance—that's love—and that's what I wanted to promise Ryan when I told him I loved him. Looking at my professor and his wife, I realized that the way I felt about Ryan in the beginning of our relationship wasn't love. It wasn't total acceptance, sacrifice, and commitment; it was intrigue and attraction. I liked Ryan, but I still had so much more to learn about him.

As one of my favorite scholars, C. S. Lewis, wrote, "Love as distinct from 'being in love' . . . is not merely a feeling. It is a deep unity, maintained by the will and deliberately strengthened by habit; reinforced by (in Christian marriages) the grace which both partners ask, and receive, from God. They can have this love for each other even at those moments when they do not like each other; as you love yourself even when you do not like yourself."

One time Ryan visited me in Chicago, and we took the train to the airport together when it was time for him to leave. There were light flurries in the air and a dusting of snow on the ground. A band played Christmas jazz music in Departures and Arrivals. Family members and friends were hugging and greeting each other, while Christmas lights strung throughout the airport set the perfect ambience for an "I love you." During that trip, Ryan and I had an amazing time together, and I was really tempted to say, "I love you," but I didn't. After he left, I took the train back home, wondering the whole time whether or not I should have gone ahead and said it. Then my phone beeped with a text from Ryan, telling me how much fun he'd had. He wrote, "You are the best of the best to me. Being with you is so easy, I never want to leave." Over the next few years I must have reread that message hundreds of times. It captured the moment better than saying "I love you" could have.

When I finally told Ryan that I loved him on our wedding day, it felt amazing to say it while feeling completely confident that I was ready to back those words up with a lifetime of sacrifice, commitment, and acceptance. And knowing the full level of commitment behind his words when I heard him say, "I love you," assured me that Ryan found me worthy of all those things too.

One Question to Ask Yourself: Who or what has defined love for you?

One Thing to Remember: Love is a choice.

One Thing to Work On: Practice agape love by doing something kind for someone in your life who you don't love or even like.

9

Creating Culture

"But as for me and my household, we will serve the LORD."

—Joshua 24:15

MY DREAM MARRIAGE

Amanda

Early in our marriage, Ryan and I were speaking to a group of young adults when a girl stood up and said, "I don't want to get married because all my married friends are unhappy." This is something we often hear. A friend recently told us, "You two are the only married couple I know that seems truly happy." While this shocked us at first, we realized that some young people think they know exactly what marriage looks like, and it's often an ugly image.

The truth is that marriage is much more complicated than many young people realize. There are many different kinds of happy marriages, and only the two people in a marriage know the reality of how ugly or beautiful it really is. Ryan and I decided that people need a new picture of what marriage can be—not the picture they grew up observing, but the beautiful new picture they can create in their own lives.

Whether or not your parents were happily married, you likely have fixed ideas about what marriage looks like. We have one friend who never saw his parents fight, not once in twenty-nine years. Now whenever he argues with his girlfriend, he assumes their relationship isn't going to work out. He thinks a good marriage means having no disagreements whatsoever. Of course, the girl he marries isn't going to have the exact same picture. She might believe that arguments are a healthy part of any good relationship. Ryan and I grew up in vastly different families, but we worked together to create the image of the marriage we wanted to share. It's time for you to create your own picture of the marriage you want. Instead of copying the picture of your family or the family your boyfriend or girlfriend grew up with, you have the chance to start fresh with an empty canvas and create a picture of what marriage is going to look like for the two of you.

Because of our unique wedding story, I didn't spend a minute actually planning our wedding, but I did spend plenty of time dreaming about it. Whenever I needed a break from studying, I went online and looked at dresses, rings, centerpieces, and floral arrangements, imagining the magical day when Ryan and I would be married. Our culture celebrates weddings on the pages of magazines, in reality shows, and especially in movies, but what about the marriage itself? Pinterest has a page called "My Dream Wedding," where I posted over two hundred images, but there's no page on Pinterest called "My Dream Marriage." A wedding is one day, but a marriage should be for life, and it needs to be planned with at least as much thought, time, and care as the wedding—if not far more.

When I was young, it was impossible for me to imagine what I wanted in a marriage because I didn't know how good marriage could be. Instead, I thought about what I didn't want, which was all around me. It wasn't until I was twenty years old that I first saw a healthy marriage between a beautiful couple, Dave and Stephanie.

The first thing I noticed about them was the way Dave honored his wife. Even before I met Stephanie, I felt like I knew her because of the way Dave talked about her and demonstrated grace through her. He talked about what first drew him to Steph—her kind heart and sweet spirit. Where I grew up, if you asked a husband what "drew him to his wife," he would likely respond, "She was fine!" I'd never heard a husband talk about his wife the way Dave did, and it struck me that Dave really knew Stephanie before he married her. Once I saw them together, I was even more inspired by the way they did everything as a team, from dividing household tasks to managing the finances and taking care of the kids. Right away, I knew that I wanted that feeling of being half of something.

OUR CORE VALUES

If God brings a couple into your life that you can aspire to be like, pull from them, but don't just imitate what you see in them. God has no interest in copying and pasting someone else's dream marriage onto yours. God has a huge plan for your relationship, and you don't want to miss it. In order to see clearly what God has in store for you, you have to start with a fresh canvas. This is your chance to figure out your core values, which will determine the culture of your future marriage. How do you want people to feel one day when they walk into your home? What are the things you prioritize above all else? What values do you want to instill in your children? What makes you tick? Here are some of the core values that have helped Ryan and me create a healthy culture in our young marriage.

Faith

If God is the Lord of your life, that means He governs every part of your life, including your love life, not just the areas that you choose. If you're interested in dating someone who doesn't share your commitment to God, it may not seem like a big deal right now. But if you're a strong Christian, your faith is a part of who you are, and that is huge.

When Ryan and I were on our break, I went on a date with a guy who had come to my college to play basketball and had just accepted Christ. As his friend, I was able to see his transformation firsthand, and that was really cool. It was also empowering because at the time I knew so much more about the Bible than he did, and he thought my knowledge was amazing. I'll admit it felt good to be seen that way!

We had fun, but when we were together, I seemed to keep bumping up against a glass wall. I couldn't explain everything to him about my relationship with Christ because I knew he wouldn't understand. He didn't do anything wrong, but he hadn't seen what I'd seen or experienced what I'd experienced. I knew he'd get there, and I was excited for him, but I couldn't get there with him. Because we were in such different places spiritually, I found myself holding back an incredibly important piece of myself, and I knew I could never marry someone who didn't know the whole me.

Think about how it might feel to marry someone you can't reveal your true self to. You may not mind setting your spiritual life aside for a little while when you're dating, but if you marry that person, you'll have to lock that piece of you away or simply let it go. Have you really accepted Christ and nurtured a relationship with Him only to throw it away? If you can't reveal your whole self to the one you're dating now, that won't change once you get married. On the other hand, being on the same page in all facets of faith can make a marriage stronger and easier. Ryan and I will always encourage each other to forgive someone who's wronged us, exercise grace, and give to others because it's part of our walk with Christ. I can tell him anything about my relationship with Christ, and I'm not afraid of how he'll respond because I know he'll understand.

Family

An important part of your future marriage's culture is the relationships you'll share with your extended family. In Matthew 19:5, the Bible talks about untying yourself from your family and cleaving to your spouse. This is important, but no matter how old you are or how far away you may live, your family and your spouse's family will still be important pieces of the culture you create together. If you're dating and even if you're single, the two steps that you should start thinking about now are setting boundaries with your family and developing relationships with the family of the person you're dating. It may seem early to be thinking about this, but I think it's important to start this process long before getting married.

When Ryan and I started getting serious, I flew home to have this important conversation with my mom. I told her in a kind, nonconfrontational way, "I'm getting older and I'm going to be making more decisions for myself. This doesn't mean you're any less a part of my life, and I still love you." I knew that Ryan and I were on the path toward marriage, and I didn't want to wait until we were engaged or married to begin becoming more independent. If I'd waited, there was a chance that she'd blamed Ryan if I stopped turning to her to help me make decisions after we were married. This talk was really difficult, especially given our past, but I had to put my big-girl boots on and do it, and I'm so glad I did.

Some parents have a harder time than others letting go of their children and embracing the fact that they're getting older. While many parents are thrilled to see their kids grow up and completely celebrate their moving on in life, others find letting go of their children one of the most challenging things they have to do. I knew that more than anything my mom wanted to feel like she was still an important part of my life. I found the balance by saying, "Mom, I want you to be a part of the process, but here are my nonnegotiables when it comes to me and Ryan."

No matter how much you separate yourself from your family members, they will always be a part of your life. Before getting married it's a good idea to talk to the person you're dating about your extended family and how you envision your relationship with them. This is especially important when you're crossing cultures, as Ryan and I did. My extended family is extremely close. If Ryan and I go to Chicago for any reason—it doesn't matter if we're only in town for twenty-four hours—

we'd better find a way to see my family. (Or they'll make a huge effort to come and see us.) Ryan's family is close, too, but in a different way. If we miss seeing them on a particular trip, they aren't as bothered by it. They know we'll find a way to see each other soon. This started off as a point of conflict, but over time I've become more understanding of the fact that we're not going to be able to see my family every single time, while Ryan has grown more understanding of the fact that we should at least try.

Remember that once you get married, your mate's family will be your family too. Get to know them now while you're dating, and let them get to know you. These are the people who are now your family. Learn the details about their issues and backgrounds. Does the groom's father suffer from depression? You need to know that. Did the bride's family always struggle with debt when she was growing up? Share that, too. If you think, *We're independent, so it doesn't matter,* I'm sorry, but you're wrong. When Grandpa loses his house and needs a place to live, your guest room might be the only answer. Better get to know Grandpa before you say, "I do."

Getting to know your partner's family is also a great opportunity to understand the person you're dating on a deeper level. The first time I met Ryan's parents, I immediately understood so much more about him. Ryan has always been extremely independent, and it used to bother me a bit because I wanted to feel like he needed me once in a while. Then I saw his family's dynamics. As Ryan explained earlier, his father has been ill since Ryan was a young boy. Since then, his mom has worked extremely hard outside the home while also taking care of her husband and maintaining financial security for the household, a big task that many others would crumble under. Seeing them interact, I realized Ryan felt that he needed to become independent in order to thrive in this environment. Now that I understand it, I don't fault him for his independence; I cherish it instead.

No family is perfect, but it's still important for you to embrace the family of the person you're dating, and that means the good, the bad, and the ugly. Setting boundaries early on will help you to accept them and allow them in turn to accept you. I have a guy friend who always used to tell his parents about the arguments he had with his fiancée. His parents started off really liking this girl, but since they only heard their son's side of the story (and of course weren't there when they settled their arguments), they started to have some reservations about her. The fiancée ended up feeling tension from her future in-laws, but she could never figure out why. She'd been so nice to his parents and thought they got along great. She and her fiancé argued occasionally, but they always worked it out. And, really, what couple doesn't have disagreements sometimes?

In fact, most of the arguments between my friend and his fiancée stemmed from the differences in their upbringings. Naturally, when he told his parents about these arguments, they couldn't understand his fiancée's point of view. After all, they were the ones who'd created the environment their son had grown up in. All the tension between this girl and her future in-laws could have been avoided if her fiancé hadn't shared details about their disagreements with his parents in the first place.

This process of separating from your family can be hard. But try to see this as a great opportunity to paint a new picture of what your own family life will look like once you're married. Yes, you'll be losing something—and it's okay to mourn this—but you're gaining something, too.

Finances

Ryan

Just as the things you choose to spend money on when you're single can tell you what you value, the way you treat money as a couple tells the world what you stand for. One resounding theme in Jesus's teaching is stewardship—what you do with the things you are given. Early in a relationship talk about what you value, what you'll spare no expense on, and what you don't believe holds value. This conversation will help set a healthy financial culture from the beginning.

Guys, realize that part of leading the relationship is setting the tone financially. This doesn't necessarily mean that the woman can't or shouldn't handle the finances, but I'd recommend that the male take the lead by getting a handle on how much you bring in every month and how much you spend before getting married. Break everything down by category and come up with a budget for yourself, and if you're thinking about marriage, come up with a budget for you two as a couple. If you start working on this before you get married, you'll have a better shot at sharing a healthy relationship with your finances down the road.

If you want to get married but think you can't afford it, take an even closer look at what you've been spending money on. Maybe you're saving up for a ring or a down payment on a house—that's fine. But I've heard guys who spend four hundred dollars on a PS4 say they can't afford to have a girlfriend. If this is you, then you're not valuing a relationship as much as you value your video games, and it's time to reprioritize. (I wish I had more time to play NBA 2K15, but I wouldn't have written a page in this book if I owned a game console.) You may not realize it, but you can change your value system at will. If you're not willing to make this shift, then you're probably not ready to be in a relationship.

The stress of finances is one of the main causes of divorce, but I think it's interesting that finances don't cause a lot of breakups between people who are just dating. The things that make you say, "I don't want to be with you," on a dating level are very different from the reasons people use to end a marriage. So even if you're not remotely ready to get married, you can and should create healthy financial habits now that are going to set you up for success in your future relationship.

When I first moved to Dallas I was barely making any money, but one of the first people I met was a financial advisor. I knew that if I met with him, I wasn't going to want to do anything that he told me to do, but I bit the bullet and forced myself. It was hard at first, but I've been slowly and surely building my retirement fund ever since.

Don't worry about being ready right now. If you want to be prepared in the future, just start preparing. It's up to you to become responsible and be a good steward of everything you've been given. If that means moving home with your mom to pay off your debt, then so be it. If I had a daughter, I'd rather give her away to a guy who'd done that than the one who drives a BMW he can't afford just to keep up appearances. Which of these guys is worthy of the person you want to marry? Well, that's the one that you want to be.

Amanda

My friend Madison was lucky enough to graduate from college debt free. Her mom worked at the college she was attending, so she received an employee scholarship that covered the cost of all her classes. Madison lived on campus, so she had to pay for room and board, but she worked two jobs and baby-sat on the weekends to make sure it was all paid off before she graduated. She met her husband at that same school, and the two of them planned to get married shortly after graduation. They had a beautiful wedding in San Antonio and were so happy as they drove off in a rented '57 Chevy after their nuptials.

A few months later, Madison came to visit her family in Dallas, and she and I grabbed lunch. We'd gotten married only months apart, so it was fun to catch up and talk about how our married lives were going. She and her husband were doing great, but they were working through some financial issues. Madison had grown up in a house and was hoping she and her husband would be able to buy a house of their own soon. The problem was, she hadn't realized before getting married how much school debt her husband now had. All their money was going straight to his loans. "We're a team," Madison told me, as she sat across from me at the café, "so I don't mind tackling it together. I just wish I'd had a better understanding of the situation before we got married." I gave her some encouragement, and finally she smiled. "If I'd known," she said, "maybe we wouldn't have rented that '57 Chevy!"

Setting a healthy financial culture for your relationship has to start with being honest with each other about the state of your finances before you get married. Trust me, nobody wants to be surprised on her wedding night by her spouse's student loans or credit-card debt that she's now responsible for too.

It's also valuable to talk about lifestyle in general before getting engaged or married. Another friend went all the way through college with her mom's Nordstrom's credit card. Whenever she wanted to buy new clothes, shoes, handbags, or makeup, she used that card, and her mom paid the bill. When she got engaged, her fiancé was surprised to learn about the credit card and felt a ton of pressure to provide the same lifestyle she'd grown accustomed to.

You can prevent these types of problems by talking about what kind of lifestyle you want to have before getting married or even engaged. Do you want to live in an apartment or save up and buy a big house? Are you going to be a family that goes on vacation once a year, every five months, or never? When you're talking about these things, both of you should feel comfortable meeting in the middle.

When Ryan and I got back from our honeymoon, I moved into his apartment. He'd only lived there for a few months, and it was pretty bare. I wanted to make it ours right away and felt so much pressure to have our home put together exactly the way I'd always envisioned it, like it was straight out of a magazine, and preferably all in the first month, please! During the first few months we were married, I was at Target, T.J. Maxx, and Bed Bath & Beyond more than I would like to admit. Once I sink my teeth into something, there's no stopping me, and I really wanted our place to have a wow factor and be the home I'd always dreamed of.

One night we were talking to our friends Normandy and Shirley, who moved to Miami the week of our wedding, and we told them how stressful it was getting everything for our home. Normandy laughed and said, "Guys, don't worry about that. We didn't even have a kitchen table our entire first year of marriage. Your house will be filled with stuff one day, but don't put pressure on yourself to get it all right now." He couldn't have been more right. I really just needed to get over myself! Ryan and I have our entire lives to put our home and our future together. There was no reason for us to expect to start at the finish line.

You may have an idea of what you want your own home and life-style to look like one day, and that's okay, but don't force yourself to get there now. A lot of young couples make the mistake of expecting to start out where their parents are now, but this isn't really fair. After all, they probably didn't start there either. It took them decades to get to this place. If you want the same lifestyle you grew up with, you might have to work just as long to get it. It's a great idea to talk about where you want to be in the future and how you're going to get there, but that doesn't mean you have to be there now. Being happy with where you are today and setting a realistic goal for the future is always going to help you make the most of each and every season as you work toward be-coming the one.

One Question to Ask Yourself: What do you want your future marriage to look like?

One Thing to Remember: The culture you create in your marriage will not only affect your life, but will also shape your children's lives.

One Thing to Work On: Get three blank sheets of paper. On one, write down the core values of the family you grew up in. On another, write down the core values of the family your mate grew up in. Then on the third sheet, write down the core values for the two of you together.

10

Loving Louder
Than Words

> "Let us not love in word or talk but in deed and in truth."
>
> —1 John 3:18, ESV

SHOW AND TELL

Ryan

Because we didn't say, "I love you" until our wedding day, Amanda and I were forced to use other ways to express our appreciation for each other. This led us to discover love languages, which were made popular by author Gary Chapman. In his book *The Five Love Languages,* Chapman claims that we each naturally show our love using one of five "languages": gifts, words of affirmation, quality time, acts of service, and physical touch. The language we use to show our love is also the one we're most likely to "hear." We feel loved when the person we're in a relationship with or married to shows love using the language we prefer to "speak."

It was obvious to me right away that my primary love language is gifts. Not only do I love buying presents for people to show my appreciation for them, but receiving gifts also makes me feel loved. Discovering Amanda's love language was also easy—it was all of them. Of course, she wants to spend quality time with me, and to her, quality time is a whole uninterrupted twenty-four hours or else it doesn't count. Yes, she wants me to show her some acts of service. No, the girl has never asked me to return any gift I've gotten her. Words of affirmation? Amanda needs positive feedback like it's water. And all I need to say about physical touch is, she's Puerto Rican. In her home, everyone is constantly hugging one another. (Of course, this is one of the many things I love so much about her.)

When we were first dating, it was easy for me to speak my own love language to Amanda and buy her gifts, but some of the others were difficult for me. One year when we were dating I bought her a gift every day for twelve days leading up to Christmas. I thought I was killing it, especially with my big gift for her on Christmas day—an iPad. At the time, iPads were very expensive, and there was no such thing as an iPad mini. She liked her iPad, but the next day Amanda wanted my attention, and I was distracted by a game. She got upset and asked, "Can we please spend some time together?"

It took me a little while to realize that while I may feel completely loved when someone buys me a gift, Amanda needs more than that. She didn't want things; she wanted me. This led me to start paying more attention to the ways she wanted to be loved instead of the ways I felt like showing my love for her. Now I know that she'd rather have my time than an expensive gift.

Our conversations about love languages evolved when we went back to Chapman's book and read about "love tanks." We realized that we would feel more loved, as if our love tanks were full, if the other did a better job of speaking our primary love language. Every week, we began checking in with each other to see how empty or full each of our love tanks were. That way, she could just tell me in a lighthearted way, "My quality-time love tank is running low," and I knew it was time to plan to spend some time together.

When Amanda's birthday came around that year, I was determined not to make the same mistake I'd made on Christmas. Her primary love language is words of affirmation, and that is definitely my weak point when it comes to communication. For her birthday, I went to Anthropologie and got her a really nice vase. Then I wrote a bunch of different words of affirmation down on little slips of paper, filled the vase with them, and placed a necklace at the bottom. This time, the gift reflected me, but it was tailor-made for her. And she loved it.

Romantic comedies make us think that when we hear someone say, "I love you," it will be the crescendo of our lives. But it's actually really easy to say, "I love you," even if you don't mean it. Unfortunately, some guys will say it to take things further physically with a girl. It's a lot harder to show your love by speaking your mate's love language. When we were dating, Amanda gave me gifts that took a lot of thought and understanding of who I was, like a pair of authentic Lakers shorts and a director's chair to encourage my dream of making films. That's how I knew she loved me. Not only did she speak my love language, but she also spoke it with gifts that showed how well she understood me. This paved the way for me to prove my love for her by planning the surprise wedding.

There's nothing wrong with saying, "I love you," but what if you challenged yourself to avoid saying it for thirty days while making an effort to show it every day? If you can show your love every day, you'll know that you're backing up sacrificial, willful agape love instead of just the emotional version.

FINDING THE WORDS

Amanda

When we were dating, Ryan and I didn't realize how much our relationship was benefiting from us waiting to say, "I love you." Back then, I wasn't always conscious of the moments I used more specific language and details to express how I felt about Ryan because I couldn't fall back on "I love you," but it turns out that's exactly what I was doing. Being specific gave me an opportunity to open up and be more honest and straightforward about the things I liked and appreciated about him. This is something that we continue in our marriage.

Ryan and I recently became the young-adult directors at our church. When the idea first came up, I was a bit nervous because we already have so much on our plates. I need a little downtime mixed into the excitement of our daily lives. But we went ahead anyway, and on the night of our first service, Ryan found small ways to be really attentive to me despite everything that he had going on. Throughout the night, he'd come over and put his arm around me and make sure I was okay. At the end of the night, we sat together outside, talking about how great a night it had been. "Thank you so much for what you did," I told him. He responded, "What do you mean?" I started to describe everything he'd done and why it meant so much to me. Because we already had a practice of explaining why, I was able to give him details about what he'd done that had made me feel that way.

When we were dating, I also got to learn exactly what Ryan appreciated about me, which often meant more to me than hearing the same old "I love you." When we were both living in Dallas before we got married, I was working a full-time job and going to school full time. I got overwhelmed a lot! We were both so busy that for a season Ryan and I normally only saw each other on weekends and maybe once or twice during the week, but we talked every night. I remember Ryan telling me one night before he hung up the phone, "I don't know how you do it all, but I'm so proud of you for doing it." Those words really motivated me to keep going and made me feel more appreciated and valued than hearing "I love you" ever could.

Since Ryan and I were long distance for part of our relationship, we often communicated by e-mail. We'd write each other long e-mails about our day or our week—explaining what we'd learned or experienced, encouraging each other, and telling each other what the other person said or did that week that meant a lot to us. This habit of writing each other "reflection e-mails" was borne out of necessity because of our long-distance relationship, but it turned out to be a healthy habit that we kept up even after we were living in the same city and continue even now in marriage! The act of writing something down forces us to think it through and reflect before communicating with the other person.

The habit of expressing my appreciation for Ryan in detail is something that has happily bled over into the rest of my life. Just the other day, I was thinking about my mom. I went to text her that I love her, but instead I thought, *Let me tell her exactly what led me to that thought.* So I wrote, "Thank you for pushing through as a single mom. You taught me persistence, determination, courage, and faith. I love you." She told me later that it meant the world to her.

Is there someone in your life you can express your appreciation for using more details than ever before? You don't have to be in a romantic relationship to start practicing the art of showing and telling your love.

COMMUNICATION AND CONFLICT

Ryan

Communication in a relationship goes far beyond saying (or not saying), "I love you." In fact, bad communication probably causes more disagreements in relationships than anything else. In our premarital class, Amanda and I learned a ton of helpful tips to improve our communication and strengthen our relationship. These are the ones that have helped us the most:

Understand Different Styles of Handling Conflict
People handle conflict in one of four different ways. Some people withdraw, which means shutting down and internalizing everything. Oth-

ers escalate the conflict, which means letting arguments snowball and gain momentum until they become much bigger than they were originally. Some approach conflict with a negative interpretation; they assume the other person has a hidden motive or agenda and mistakenly interpret their innocent statements as an attack. The fourth style of handling conflict is redirection, which is when you start invalidating the other person instead of dealing with the issue at hand, allowing the argument to become about something else entirely.

None of these styles are necessarily good or bad—or I should say they're all good and they're all bad. The most important thing is to be aware and understand which one the person you're dating does most. It's amazing how much simple awareness can help. From there, the best thing you can do is listen and listen well. You also need to understand your own style of handling conflict and where it came from. We all grew up watching adults argue and absorbing silent messages about how conflict should be handled, so we all have our own ideas about what is or isn't appropriate. For example, based on the noise level of the house you grew up in, you have your own idea of what constitutes yelling. If you grew up in a really loud house, you might feel like you need to shout in order to make your voice heard. But if your home was quiet, you might be sensitive to a raised voice.

This is important because so many fights happen when one person thinks the other one is yelling at them. But we often don't intend to yell; we're just repeating the patterns we saw growing up. When you meet your mate's family, pay attention to how they communicate. If you know that the person you're dating grew up in a quiet home, take pains not to raise your voice during an argument.

Get in the Mind-Set of a Loser

By this I mean stop trying to win the fight. When Amanda and I argue, I remind myself that I don't want to win the fight—I want to win her. If you sense a fight is brewing, tell the other person, "I'm all ears. For the next ten minutes, I'm going to listen to you, and at the end of this thing, I don't want to win this fight; I want you." When we find ourselves in an argument, it's natural to want be the one who's "right," to win. But forget about winning the argument and focus on winning the person. After a fight, neither of you should walk away feeling defeated *or* vindicated. You're not going to get an award or trophy for winning the argument. The person you're dating is not your opponent! Try to see this person as your teammate instead of someone you're trying to beat.

Of course, this is harder than it sounds, especially in the heat of the moment. That's why I try to get myself into the mind-set of a loser before things get heated, when there's just the slightest hint of conflict coming around the corner. That's the best time to take a pause and remind yourself what's really important.

Learn What's Important

Not long ago I found myself scrolling through my Facebook profile, and I went back all the way to the beginning, to the first few photos I posted back in 2005. In every photo, I found something to laugh at myself about as I asked, "Why did I think those clothes were cool? Why did I get that haircut? Why did I ever wear silver chains? Why was I friends with that person?" The decisions I'd made in the past (and took seriously at the time) had become comical. As I thought about how much time and energy went into those choices, I vowed to redirect both toward seeing the big picture. This has extended to all aspects of my life from the clothes I wear to the way I treat Amanda.

Think about who you were five years ago—what you wore, who you hung out with, even the music you listened to. Is there anything you did back then that makes you cringe now? Now think about yourself five years from now. What are you doing right now that you'll look back at in five years and cringe? It's silly and wasteful to spend time arguing with someone you love about things that won't seem important five years from now. When you find yourself in an argument, stop and ask yourself if this will still be important in the future. In five years, will you remember the game you wanted to go to or the text you didn't like, or will you look back and think, "I can't believe I got mad at you about that"? If it won't be important then, it's not that important now.

Keep Score (Yes, you read that right)

Most relationship experts will say to never keep score in your relationship, but I think the only way to know if you're succeeding is to keep score—not of all the bad things your partner does, but the good things. Try keeping positive scores. Start a log in your phone of special moments you've shared and the kind things you've done for each other. Some of the worst words to use in an argument are *always* and *never,* but they get said a lot because in the heat of the moment, it's easy to forget all the good things and focus on the negative. A record of wins will let you know where you're succeeding and where you have room to grow.

At all times, I have a running list in my head of things Amanda did that I want to affirm. Keeping this list present in my mind prevents me from making blanket statements that aren't true, and it holds me accountable. Sometimes when we're upset about something, it feels like we've felt this way for a long time, but the truth may be that you simply had one bad moment. Don't let that one bad moment ruin a great relationship.

When I was younger a youth pastor asked me, "How was your day?" I told him, "I'm having a bad day," and his response really changed the way I think about things. He asked, "Are you having a bad day? Or did you have a bad moment?" I thought about my whole day and realized that a lot of good things had happened, but I was letting one bad moment overshadow all of that. Too many people let one bad moment turn into a bad day that turns into a bad week that turns into a bad month that turns into a bad year that turns into what they start to envision as a bad life. You're better than that.

A record of wins will prevent one bad moment with your mate from ruining your day together. When I proposed and Amanda opened the door to the hotel to find all our friends and family there, the big win was the fact that her mother and grandfather were standing there, supporting us and offering us their blessing. That never could have happened if it weren't for all the little wins that we'd built up in our relationship, from the Lakers shorts she bought me and the "full tank" of words of affirmation I gave her to the countless other ways we've learned to show and tell each other how much we care.

One Question to Ask Yourself: What is your love language?

One Thing to Remember: We all feel and express love differently.

One Thing to Work On: Be specific about what you appreciate about the people in your life instead of relying on the words, "I love you."

11

The Comparison Trap

As they were coming home, when David returned from striking down the Philistine, the women came out of all the cities of Israel, singing and dancing, to meet King Saul, with tambourines, with songs of joy, and with musical instruments. And the women sang to one another as they celebrated, "Saul has struck down his thousands, and David his ten thousands." And Saul was very angry, and this saying displeased him. He said, "They have ascribed to David ten thousands, and to me they have ascribed thousands, and what more can he have but the kingdom?" And Saul eyed David from that day on.

—1 Samuel 18:6–9, ESV

GREAT EXPECTATIONS

Ryan

Soon after Amanda and I posted "The Surprise Wedding" video, I got an e-mail from a guy named Chad. He wrote, "I have a major concern about setting expectations so high. What if a guy couldn't do this original kind of thing and his fiancée is dreaming and expecting this type of Hollywood hype?" Well, in many ways Chad was right. The video captured thirty of the most romantic minutes of our entire relationship, not the five years of processing that went into it. I told Chad that all I did was listen to my girlfriend and do my best, and that's exactly what I encourage others to do. Amanda could have said that she wanted everyone at our wedding to wear costumes, and I would've had everyone in costumes. I would've asked my dad if he'd rather be Spider-Man or Sponge Bob. Amanda just happened to want something that was YouTube-ish, but we do things for each other all the time that mean more to us privately and will never be worthy of a YouTube documentary.

My goal in posting our wedding video online was not to be the top dog when it comes to proposals. Instead, I wanted to inspire people to give their all to their own love story, no matter how much or how little that may be. But it's not that surprising that the wedding video did turn into a competition when so many of us allow other people's lives and relationships to make us feel jealous or insecure about our own.

We all feel a certain amount of pressure to live up to expectations that have been set for us by our parents, our church, or even our society. During our momentum years when we're going through a lot of transitions, we constantly feel the pressure to move on to the next phase of life. When you're single, the questions are, "Why are you single, and when are you going to start dating?" When you're dating, it's, "When are you going to get married?" When you're living in an apartment, it's, "When are you going to buy a house?" And when you're married and in a house, it's, "When are you going to have kids?"

We have this constant pressure to upgrade our cars, careers, and social status. Where does it end? We see our friends not only hitting those milestones but also buying each other lavish gifts, going on dream vacations, and looking as if they're perfectly happy all the time, and we start to feel that our relationships aren't any good if our entire lives aren't one amazing moment after another. This is what we call the comparison trap, and it's completely toxic for relationships.

The idea of jealousy or comparisons is nothing new—it goes all the way back to the Bible—but social media has heightened our awareness. Before, I would have to go to someone's house to see how he's living, but now all I have to do is check my news feed. Too often what we see on social media, at a party, or even on Sunday at church in no way reflects what's really going on in someone's life. So many times I've seen a picture posted by a smiling and hugging couple and then, five minutes later, listened when they called and said they're in the middle of a fight. The same couples show up to church in their Sunday best for one main reason—to keep up appearances. We all want to give the impression that we're happy. It's embarrassing to admit to any weakness, especially publicly. That's why you see people tweeting pictures of gifts, vacations, and nights out instead of a status like, "We're having issues tonight; pray for us."

None of us wants to be the person who cheated or the one who can't get along with his spouse. If you're feeling down about your relationship and post a picture of the two of you looking cute, you feel better when people post positive comments. Deep down I think many of us believe that if we tell the world that we're happy, then maybe we really will be happy. But when others compare their real life with your fake happiness, they'll always come up short. Some of my friends have told me that they think all I do is go to NBA games. That's obviously not true—it's just what they see on my news feed. As Dave Ramsey says, "Never compare someone else's highlight reel with your behind-the-scenes footage."

When you're using social media, it's a good practice to ask yourself, "Why am I posting this?" You're the only person who really knows the truth, and if there's a hidden agenda behind your posts, take some time to think about why it's important to you to send that message. At the end of the day, we're all doing a little bit of self-marketing. We're putting something out there that tells the world we're okay. But what would happen if we stopped marketing ourselves on social media and started being a little more honest? I'm not talking about airing all your dirty laundry; I'm suggesting making your social media accounts a more authentic representation of your life, your struggles, and your ups and downs. I believe this would allow us all to affirm one another's situations, and we'd all feel a little bit better about ourselves if we could easily see that we're all really going through similar things.

I intentionally became a loser about a year ago, and it was one of the greatest days of my life. This meant simply looking at all the people I'd been comparing myself to and saying, "I don't need to have anything nicer than you. You have the better story and the cooler stuff. You win. I lose." We all want a newer car, a nicer wardrobe, and a bigger house, but what would it feel like to surrender your need for those things and seek to find contentment with what you already have? To me, that's the only way to really win.

Continually having your eye on someone else will keep you from being everything God has called you to be. Saul is the perfect example of what happens when you fall for the comparison trap. What Saul couldn't know is that the Bible describes him as "the most handsome man in Israel—head and shoulders taller than anyone else in the land" (1 Samuel 9:2, NLT). Now, there are many great patriarchs of the faith in the Old and New Testament: Abraham, Noah, Moses, Elijah, Peter, Paul, and so on, but none of them received a compliment like this. It's one thing for *People* magazine to say you're the most handsome man in the land, but if the Bible says it, that means you were really a stud!

The problem is, Saul didn't realize how amazing he was because he had his eye on someone else. First Samuel 18:9 tells us, "And Saul eyed David from that day on" (ESV). Who knows what would have happened to Saul if he'd stopped comparing himself to David? The course of history would have been altered if David and Saul had joined forces instead of competing. We can always do more together than we can individually. Saul wasted resources, time, and energy trying to chase and kill David instead of experiencing what could have been one of the most kingly reigns in history with David by his side. We will always fail to see who we are when we're busy looking at others. What are you missing out on because you're busy trying to compete with someone else?

COURTING CONTENTMENT

I'll admit it: about six years ago I fell into the comparison trap. For two years, I made it my goal not to wear the same outfit twice because I wanted to be known as the best-dressed guy around. I know, I know, but look—I made some bizarre choices in my day too, just as you may have. It was all about the image I portrayed; none of those clothes actually made me happy. Trying to win everybody over like this cost me an insane amount of time and money, and it didn't allow anyone to truly know me. When you're on the road to marriage, you're on your way to being fully known. So how can you ever expect to have a happy marriage when you're busy trying to keep up appearances?

Back then I didn't have contentment. I was thirsty, desperate, and willing to go to great lengths to get a thing, and when you're in that place, there's no amount that can ever be enough. Is there a number of dollar bills or square footage or retweets that will make you happy? If you're not content with what you have today and you can't name the number that will make you happy, you'll never have enough. If the number is just whatever will impress your friends, you'll be chasing that number for the rest of your life. New houses are built every year, and the status quo will always be changing. As the target keeps moving, you'll be left chasing a carrot on a stick. To be content, you have to move that target inward.

Some of the most frequently quoted words from the Bible are Paul's in Philippians 4:13: "I can do all things through Christ who strengthens me" (NKJV). But I think the more important words come just before this verse, "I know what it is to be in need, and I know what it is to have plenty. I have learned the secret of being content in any and every situation, whether well fed or hungry, whether living in plenty or in want." (Philippians 4:12, NIV.) How is Paul able to make this iconic statement that he could do all things through Christ? Where does he get that? He gets it from contentment, and he tells us that he's not going to allow his circumstances to determine his success. It's from a place of contentment that he realizes Christ is the only source of the strength he needs to accomplish great things.

When you're thirsty, you're looking for someone else to satisfy and fulfill you, but that will never happen. The most attractive person of the opposite sex is always going to be the one who doesn't need you, who's already operating from a place of contentment. That's probably the number one thing that attracted me to Amanda. I was an added bonus to her life, but she was content without me. It took time for me to grow to be content, and it wasn't until I got there, that I was ready for a relationship with Amanda. First, I had to be okay with possibly disappointing girls by saying, "I wore the same shirt twice this week." It's dumb; I know.

The Bible tells us that the prodigal son was thirsty and searching when he left and spent his inheritance on foolish things. When he returned, the older brother, who had spent the years his brother was missing working by his father's side, was jealous of the reception his brother received. He went out to the fields and sulked instead of going to the party, too busy comparing how his father treated him and his brother to join in the celebration. (See Luke 15:11–32).

Too often, we make the same mistake. We view other's accomplishments and get sucked into the comparison trap instead of joining the party and celebrating someone else's success. Try to stop comparing yourself to others and start celebrating them, instead. Congratulating people on their accomplishments costs you nothing, and these tiny gestures can help you feel connected.

If we're going to connect with one another, I think we're going to connect more on our weaknesses than our strengths. Being honest and vulnerable about your life will also make it easier to lean on others when you're facing a real problem because you'll be coming to them from an equal place instead of from up on a throne. We all want to be superheroes, but this is dangerous because it keeps people from believing that you need them. Remember, Clark Kent had friends and a girlfriend, while Superman was always left alone. Be a loser. Be Clark Kent. And you'll win every time.

FINDING SECURITY WITHIN

Amanda

My friend Alex is one of the most secure people I know. She has an inner confidence about her that isn't about ego or bragging rights; she's just extremely comfortable with who she is and knows her worth. Alex is the first one to celebrate someone else's life without wasting one minute feeling jealous or insecure, and she shines from within with joy and contentment.

When Alex was fifteen her father asked her on a date—her first date. He asked for her mom's permission to take her out and then rented a car, brought her flowers, and rang the doorbell when it was time to "pick her up." Alex had bought a new dress and done her hair and was so excited to go with her dad to a fancy restaurant in downtown Chicago. Over dinner her dad told Alex, "You've become such a beautiful young lady, and I want you to know what you deserve. The next time someone rings our doorbell and wants to date you, if he shows you any less than this amount of effort, this amount of respect, and this amount of honor, you'll know that he is not the right person for you."

Alex's first date set the bar for every guy she met. After that, if one of them came to pick her up and beeped the horn from the street, she knew that maybe they could be friends, but that wasn't the guy for her. She never settled, and she ended up marrying her best friend. Throughout her entire wedding day, her dad wore a picture of Alex as a little girl giving her dad a kiss pinned to his suit jacket. He wanted everyone, especially his new son-in-law, to know who was her first love.

Right now one in three American children are living without a father in their home. That's about 15 million kids who don't have a father present, and that doesn't include all the children who have fathers who are physically present but emotionally absent. I wouldn't call that a shocking statistic, as I think most of us are familiar with it, but it is alarming, and I believe that our generation's "fatherlessness" has made us far more likely to fall into the comparison trap. I would never discount a mother's role in a child's life, but there's something really special about affirmation from a father. I know from experience that when you grow up without that, you're always seeking, always thirsty, always looking to fill a void within you. You're covertly hankering for someone to affirm that you did a good job, that you made a good decision, that *you are enough.*

APPEARANCES VERSUS REALITY

Humans have always looked around and gauged how they were doing based on comparisons. What social media has done is take the images we're most likely to come up short against and put them right at our fingertips. In the past I could have seen an image of Jennifer Aniston sporting beautiful designer shoes that my Target heels only wish they could be someday. Then as soon as I turned off the TV, I might have realized, *Oh, she has a bunch of money and a personal stylist who hand-picks her shoes,* and the thought would fade away. But now, I pick up my phone and see my friend who lives ten minutes away wearing new Christian Louboutin sling-backs with a six-inch heel, and this time, it's personal.

These comparisons don't just happen on social media. They happen at school, in youth groups, and even among friends. Before girl-friends get together in a group, they often spend more time planning their outfits than they would for a date! Then over brunch, instead of sharing the nitty-gritty details about their work and relationship struggles, they often claim, "Everything is great." This is all an effort to impress and one-up each other instead of being authentic and honest about what's going on.

What does this have to do with relationships? Well, our relationship status is one thing we all feel insecure about sometimes. If you're single, you might be all fired up about your purpose as a single person, but all it takes is hearing about the way a friend's boyfriend surprised her with flowers to make you to think, *Huh. I wish someone bought me flowers.* Even this is all smoke and mirrors. For all you know, he bought her those flowers because they had a horrible fight last night. If you get into a relationship just to get some flowers (or to get whatever someone else has), you'll never be fulfilled.

Even once you're in a relationship, it's easy to feel insecure about your status if you spend too much time comparing yourself to others. I've fallen on both sides of this coin. After "The Surprise Wedding" video started getting a lot of attention, Ryan and I went on *The Queen Latifah Show*. They announced, "This time Amanda has a surprise for Ryan, and it's Kobe Bryant!" This was an amazing moment, but listen, I never called Kobe Bryant. I never walked door to door asking people to sign a petition so my husband could meet Kobe Bryant. Sure, when the *Queen Latifah* producers asked me if I could think of a surprise for Ryan, I pushed hard for it to be Kobe, but I had an entire staff and a celebrity helping me make it happen. When the show aired, it was fascinating and a little strange to hear guys say, "Amanda wins the best wife award," or "I wish my girl would do something like that for me."

But even being on that side of things and knowing that things aren't always how they appear hasn't stopped me from falling into the comparison trap myself. When I saw that one of my friends had gotten her boyfriend Dallas Cowboys tickets and a helicopter ride for his birthday, I thought, "Oh my gosh, all I got Ryan was some trendy dress socks." Instead of being happy for them, I was focused on how my gift stacked up. Think about how quickly your perspective of your own relationship can change just by comparing it to someone else's. If your boyfriend buys you a dozen roses, you may be thrilled, but if you find out that a friend's boyfriend bought her a dozen roses for every room in the house, suddenly your puny one dozen doesn't seem so great. You might even equate his buying her more roses with him loving and caring about her more, but none of that is true or real.

If you find yourself falling for the comparison trap, the best thing you can do is refocus. Not too long ago Ryan and I heard a pastor talk about the saying "Count your blessings." This phrase has become a cliché meaning "Remember to be grateful," but this pastor said, "Have you ever really counted your blessings? I mean naming them one by one?" Ryan and I were lying in bed that night when he said, "Did you hear what the pastor said this morning? Have you ever done that before?" I told him that I hadn't, and he said, "Let's do it." I agreed, and Ryan continued, "Let's start with our jobs, our house, our clothes." I chimed in, "Our friends, our families, all of the opportunities we've been given."

We continued to go back and forth for a few minutes, pausing every so often to stare up at the ceiling in wonder. "Man, this is crazy," Ryan said after a while. We couldn't believe we were still going. "I'm so glad my mom beat cancer," I said. "I'm grateful that we're thriving in this first year of marriage," Ryan commented. "I'm glad we have money in our bank account," I added, "even if it's not as many zeros as we'd like!" We both knew we still weren't completely done, but we'd gotten the point. By then, we were both in awe, and we lay there silently for a while as I fought back tears, completely overwhelmed with gratitude for how much God has blessed us.

If you're single, thank God that you're not in an unhealthy relationship. If you're in a relationship, thank God for the fact that you have a faithful partner or an encouraging partner. You fill in the blanks. The dozens of roses your friend got will seem so small when you compare them to the greater things in life, like love, encouragement, faithfulness, and friendship.

Sometimes refocusing isn't enough. A few years ago, I had a habit of opening the Facebook app on my phone every morning before even getting out of bed. I told myself that I was just taking a minute to let my brain wake up, but the truth is that I'd grown attached to seeing what other people's lives were like and using them to gauge whether or not mine was good enough. I scrolled through with an internal dialogue in my head: *That's dumb. That's stupid. Oh, that's cute. What is that?* I was judging everything. I'd get to one person's selfie and think, *She's pretty,* and then before I knew it I was stalking all her pictures to find out if she was really that pretty or if it was just that one photo. Don't leave me hanging here; I know you've done this too!

It was a trap, and I totally fell for it. I realized that I was putting too much stock into what I posted, wasting tons of time wondering if people would "Like" what I had to say. It was also around that time that a lot of girls I knew were getting engaged and posting all about the engagement process. I'd see, "I just said yes to the dress," with a picture of the bride-to-be with all her friends, and even though I trusted God's timing for Ryan and me, for a split second I'd feel jealous, wondering, *When do I get to say yes to the dress?*

If you're used to posting everything you do on social media, it can be oppressive to feel like you have to look your best at every moment and come up with something new and exciting to show. It's almost like we're all celebrities who might get snapped by the paparazzi when we're out getting groceries, but in this case we're our own paparazzi! Turn the camera off yourself and see how amazingly liberating it feels.

Of course, the best thing you can do to avoid falling for the comparison trap is to spend some time finding out what God thinks about you. Stop focusing on keeping up with the Leaks or whoever you have your eye on, and work on keeping up with God's image of you. One morning as I scrolled through Facebook, I realized that I had a Bible app right next to the Facebook app, just a tap of the finger away. When I got rid of Facebook and started clicking on the Bible app instead, I was able to stop comparing myself to others and find what was really important.

One Question to Ask Yourself: What are you not seeing in your relationship because your eyes are on someone else?

One Thing to Remember: It's easy to feel bad about your daily life when you're comparing it to someone else's highlights.

One Thing to Work On: Find the beauty in what God has created you to be.

12

One Vision

In everything I did, I showed you that by this kind of hard work we must help the weak, remembering the words the Lord Jesus himself said: "It is more blessed to give than to receive."

—Acts 20:35

TWO IS BETTER THAN ONE

Amanda

When Ryan and I were dating, I read James 1:27, which says to "look after widows and orphans in their distress." In my studies I'd spent a lot of time debating whether or not the Bible should be taken literally, but I knew right away there was no wiggle room or alternate way to interpret that particular verse. I called Ryan and asked him, "Do you know any widows?" Ryan was only twenty-four years old, and I'm younger than him. We knew plenty of single moms, but we didn't know any widows. Ryan called our church and asked the church secretary, "Do you know any widows? We want to help them." She paused for a moment and told Ryan, "Yes, my aunt just lost her husband, and she is drowning in medical bills."

Ryan and I decided to put some money together to send to her along with a note of encouragement. We weren't married yet and neither of us had a lot to give her, but we realized that it added up to a lot more when both of us contributed than if either of us had given by ourselves. After we sent out the check and card, we didn't really think about it again until we went back to church. As soon as she saw us come in, the church secretary stopped us. "Your kindness meant so much to my aunt," she told us. "It was really timely for her. She was able to pay off a few bills, and your encouragement meant the world." The fact that she was addressing Ryan and me together as a unit, and not one or the other of us, really struck me. I realized in that moment that we could use our relationship to help the people around us. Together we could make a far greater impact than either of us could alone.

That experience opened our eyes to the needs of others, whether they were widows, orphans, or just people who were struggling financially or needed encouragement. We each started keeping an ear out for people who needed something, and every so often Ryan or I would approach the other and say, "My friend needs some help. Let's send something." I have a heart for single moms after seeing my mom work so hard to raise my brother and me alone, so I was always on the lookout for single moms we could help. I'd become friends with a single mom at my school who was struggling financially, so Ryan and I got together and sent her some money.

I had another friend who was married with two kids, and she and her husband were having a hard time making ends meet. Ryan and I put some money together, and I asked her to meet me at my dorm. She thought something was wrong until she showed up and I handed her the card and check. "This is from me and Ryan," I told her. "We really want to bless you guys." She looked at the check and said, "No, I can't accept this." I made sure to tell her, "It's not just us giving this to you. God placed you on our hearts. He hasn't forgotten about you."

Until we started doing this, I'd been busy focusing on getting through college and my own financial struggles. I didn't know how I was going to make it and never imagined that I could spare anything to help somebody else, but opening my eyes to needs around me helped me see that there were other people out there who had far greater struggles than I did. And if I really tried, I was always able to find a few extra dollars to give to someone who needed them more.

We didn't realize it in the moment, but every time we teamed up to bless someone, it strengthened our own relationship. We built up confidence in each other as we saw over and over that we could accomplish so much more together than we could separately. Before we got married, everyone warned us that selfishness was the one thing that could destroy a marriage. Being married means putting someone else's needs above your own, and that is the very definition of generous. By learning to be generous with others, Ryan and I had unknowingly set up a healthy habit of generosity that translated into all facets of our relationship. Generosity gave us a purpose, something to stand for that is bigger and more significant than just the two of us.

A VISION FOR YOUR FAMILY

While we were dating, Ryan taught a leadership course and spoke about how businesses should create vision statements. I thought this was a great idea, and I told him, "Let's do our own." We started creating a vision statement for our future family. At first, it was just a note in our phones, but I dreamed of getting it blown up to hang on the wall of our family home one day. Our mission statement evolved over time. Today it reads, "At our house, we honor God. We love hard. We don't take ourselves too seriously. We give because it's better than receiving. We welcome people in. We respond to needs. We see the best in everyone." This is a work in progress. In the beginning, it simply read, "We respond to needs," and we realized that our main priority was to be generous to others.

Since then, we've tried to live up to our mission statement in many different ways. There have been plenty of times when we knew someone was struggling and sent a simple note of encouragement along with a ten-dollar Starbucks card. Nearly every time we did this, the person responded by saying, "I really needed that this week." Sometimes the encouragement we offered made a greater impact than any amount of money we could have given. One couple we're friends with got married when Ryan and I were still dating, and they were having a really hard time communicating. They were fighting all the time, and it pained us to see this. They had so much potential, but they were young and didn't know a lot about relationships.

Ryan and I weren't even engaged (or married) yet, but we'd done so much work to learn about relationships, and we wanted them to spend some time around people who knew a little differently than they did. We started inviting them over to hang out every so often just so they could witness our own interactions and see how we operated as a team. So much of what we'd learned about communication came from our premarital class, so we encouraged them to sign up, but they couldn't afford the fee. We knew how much they'd benefit from it, so we signed them up for the class and paid for it. They learned a lot, and when we saw them recently, they were doing so much better than ever before.

Another friend is a single mom who was going to school at night when Ryan and I first got married, and she couldn't afford childcare. I offered to watch her little girl two nights a week while my friend was in school. I knew it was a lot to ask of Ryan so early in our marriage to have a little girl in our house taking up my attention, but by then we'd built up so much confidence in each other that I knew he'd understand. We saw it as a blessing that this little girl was able to spend time hanging out with me and Ryan and seeing a healthy marriage in action.

One of Ryan's best friends, Phil, recently called Ryan and told him about a conversation he had with another one of our friends who'd asked about what we did for a living and our financial situation. Phil told Ryan that he'd responded, "You could never calculate how much they make because they give so much of it away." While at first it made me feel a little bit uncomfortable to know someone was asking about our finances, I quickly realized that this was exactly what we'd want to be known for. Ever since creating our vision statement, Ryan and I had been striving to live up to it without realizing that anyone else noticed, but Phil noticed. The way he described us matched with that vision statement, and that meant that we were on the right path.

Ecclesiastes 4:9 tells us, "Two are better than one, because they have a good return for their labor." When I heard Phil talking about Ryan and me that way, it was a big win for us because he wasn't talking about me individually or Ryan individually. He was talking about *us,* and cultivating an *us* mentality solidifies the idea that two is indeed better than one. Every relationship and every marriage needs reminders that you're good together and that you can *do* good together. Ryan has his private victories that I celebrate, and I have my own private victories that he celebrates, but those celebrations can't compare to the ones we celebrate when we've done something together that worked.

After our first year of marriage came to a close and we looked back, we realized that it had been much easier than we'd heard and feared it would be. We definitely had our share of disagreements, but it didn't feel as hard or stressful as our friends and families had cautioned us it would. One night we were sitting together on the couch when I asked Ryan, "Why do you think the past year has been so much easier than we thought it would be?" We talked through it for a few minutes. "We'd already practiced generosity together for years before getting married," Ryan said with his giant grin. "It's become a part of our DNA."

When you give something away that you wish you could hold on to, it shaves a little bit of selfishness off of you. The first time Ryan and I teamed up to give money away to the church secretary's aunt, my portion was only fifty dollars while Ryan gave a hundred. That's all we could give at the time. One hundred and fifty dollars is a drop in the bucket to a widow with a ton of medical bills to pay, but to a college student like me, fifty dollars was everything! I could have gotten a manicure and pedicure or treated myself to Starbucks every day for a month, and with his hundred dollars Ryan could have bought another pair of shoes. But if we'd kept that money, would Ryan still be wearing those shoes today? Would that manicure still be on my fingers? And more important, did either of us really need these things? Obviously, the answer to all of these questions is no.

Every time Ryan and I gave a small amount of money away or showed up for someone to support them when we could've been doing something for ourselves, it opened our eyes a little bit more to other people's needs. By the time we got married, our eyes were wide open to each other's needs, and that made it easier to always think of the other person and put that person first. After all the giving we'd already done, it wasn't a big deal to order the pizza Ryan wanted when I was craving Mexican. We knew by then that people are what matter, not things.

Once you're in a serious relationship, starting to build a vision statement for your own relationship and perhaps for your future family is a great idea. Two people coming from different backgrounds will almost always have different expectations of how their home and family will operate. Putting a vision statement down on paper gives you a goal to strive for. If you don't know what you're aiming for, how will you ever reach it? When you have a goal, you have accountability. If you write on your vision statement that you are a family who forgives, you'll be motivated and inspired to forgive each other and those around you every day. Otherwise, what will you say when your future child watches you holding a grudge against your mate and asks, "Mom, I thought in this family we forgive"?

If you're in a relationship, take some time to sit together and create a vision statement. Do it together instead of one of you doing it and running it by the other. As you work it out on paper, you'll be working it out in your relationship, too. Your vision statement doesn't have to be about generosity. That's just what felt right to Ryan and me. In a lot of Christian homes, you see this verse from Joshua: "As for me and my household, we will serve the LORD." This is a great start for a vision statement, but what does it mean practically speaking? To Ryan and me, serving the Lord means loving even when we don't want to, forgiving others, and being generous. A great place to begin creating your own vision statement is to ask yourself what it means to you to serve the Lord.

We have seen some of our friends use their own marriages to accomplish amazing things that reflect their own vision statements. Our friends Phil and Audrey are big on hospitality. When we visit them, they go far out of their way to make sure we have everything we need. The last time they were at our house, they silently noticed our favorite food and drinks, and when we showed up at their house months later, the fridge was stocked with that stuff. Phil and Audrey are youth pastors, and their hospitality shines through their kids. When a new person comes to their youth group, their kids will do whatever they can to make sure the new person is comfortable. I didn't know Audrey very well before she and Phil got married, but I did know that hospitality was a huge part of Phil's DNA, so I was happy to learn that Audrey came from an Italian background and grew up in a very hospitable family. It's been amazing to see it blossom between the two of them together. Like Ryan and me, Phil and Audrey can do so much more together than they ever could have on their own.

I'd describe our friends Alishia and David as a couple that shows up for other people. They're always there when one of their friends needs something, no matter how unglamorous the task at hand may be. At our wedding, Alishia walked back and forth across the flood bringing flowers from one venue to another. When we moved recently, they're the only couple who called us and asked for the details about our move, and then said, "We'll be there after work." Without us even asking, David came over in his work clothes and helped move our stuff. They say you know who your real friends are when moving day comes. Can I get an amen?! Alishia and David were also the first ones to excitedly share our "Surprise Wedding" video and the first ones to offer to throw us a baby shower when we announced that we were expecting!

Your turn. How would your vision statement for your future family read? What can you accomplish together that will be better and more meaningful than what either of you could do alone?

Wisdom Versus Faith

Ryan

In so many circles, we Christians are known for what we don't do: we don't go to see a certain type of movie, we don't have sex before marriage, we don't swear, and we don't listen to certain kinds of music. It's easy to spend your days carefully avoiding certain things, but what if you started focusing on the things you do instead of the things you don't do? If you're on a journey toward becoming the one, you can decide right now what you're going to be known for. Will you be the person who simply followed all the rules or the one who followed all the rules because your life was so full of purpose?

I didn't grow up having a lot. I knew how I felt whenever I got a gift or someone paid for my food, and I saw how people reacted when someone else encouraged them. What I realized over time was that about nine out of the ten people I wrote encouragement letters to responded by saying, "I really needed that." So I adopted the philosophy that 90 percent of us need encouragement. I started writing letters of encouragement to friends every week and using whatever means I had to help those in need. I knew even then that people like those who are generous, and I'll admit I wanted to be liked. Not only have I never wanted for friends since then, but I've also never been bored. For years I practiced generosity, and over time giving to others became my thing. Now it's part of my DNA; it's what I do, and I pray that it'll be what I'm remembered for.

When I was a very young child, my father taught me about the concept of tithing—giving 10 percent of your income to the church. I grew up watching my parents tithe, and ever since I started earning money by mowing lawns in middle school, I've been a tither. I've never known a time when this wasn't something I strongly believed in. Of course, it was sometimes difficult for me to hand money over because I had so little.

The surprise wedding cleared out my bank account. Though I'd carefully budgeted, and Amanda and I had both saved up to pay for a wedding, there were still unexpected expenses. To make matters worse, I'd barely worked for several weeks leading up to the wedding because I was so busy with the preparations. Amanda and I considered ourselves extremely blessed to have been able to pay for the wedding ourselves and to have such flexible work situations, but when we got back from our honeymoon, I saw that my bank account had ten dollars in it.

I had no idea what we were going to do or how we were going to make those ten dollars stretch until my next paycheck came. Amanda and I had been married for all of a week. I couldn't tell her that we had only ten dollars to our names because I didn't want her to worry or feel guilty about spending all our money on the wedding. I trusted that God would provide for us, so I stayed calm, didn't say anything, and acted like everything was fine. Amanda and I went to church that day, and as always, I tithed. "Lord," I said, as I handed over one of my very last dollars, "I trust you. I know you'll provide for us."

The next day I looked at my bank account online and saw that it contained an extra $1,700. I assumed it was a mistake, but when I clicked on the deposit, I learned that it was from the Diplomat Resort and Spa near Miami where we'd gotten married. I called the Diplomat and spoke to the catering manager I'd been working with for over a year. "There must be a mistake," I told him. "It looks like you deposited $1,700 into my account."

"No mistake," he told me. "It's a refund. It looks like we accidentally overcharged you for a few things. Plus, we're sorry about the rain." I was shocked. "Thank you," I said and hung up, feeling overwhelmed with the sense that God was looking over me and Amanda. I knew in that moment that, no matter what, we'd be taken care of.

If you have ten dollars in your bank account, it may not seem like the best idea to give one penny of it away, but I knew in my heart that's what God wanted me to do. I definitely didn't practice wisdom in every area concerning the wedding; that's why I was left with only ten dollars in my bank account. But at that moment I trusted my faith and God's wisdom above my own, and that's always the wisest move. Wisdom and faith can sometimes be at odds with each other. Some of the things Jesus asked His disciples to do may not seem like the best ideas if you think about them practically. It's never wise to get out of a boat in the middle of a storm and try to walk on water. That's not smart—that's ludicrous, but that's what Jesus asked them to do.

When He sent His disciples out two by two on their first mission trip in Matthew 10, He told them to leave their wallets and bags behind. Now, that's just crazy. How were they supposed to eat? And don't forget—Jesus wasn't going with them. He was staying behind, and He sent them out empty-handed. But in Luke 22 He asked them if they lacked anything, and the answer was no. Food, shelter, and clothing were provided everywhere they went. God worked it out—and He always does.

In Acts 20:35 the Bible tells us that it is more blessed to give than to receive. This phrase is repeated so often that it has become a cliché, but I still think it's a hard pill for many of us to swallow. In order to really absorb this message, you need to change your perspective. Take a moment to ask yourself right now if deep down, you truly believe it's better to give or to receive. If there's a part of you that thinks it's better to receive, ask yourself one more question—is it better to make a million dollars or to give away a million dollars? A lot of people immediately assume it's better to make or receive a million dollars, but the truth is that if you were to give away a million dollars, you'd have to earn even more than that. I tell people to change their companies' goal from making a million dollars in the next year to giving away a million dollars. In order to give away a million dollars, they'd have to be making a whole lot more. Think bigger than you ever have before. It *is* better to give than to receive because the person who's in a position to give is always mighty blessed to be there.

SHOWING UP

When my dad had his first stroke years go, he was a pastor in the city and had tons of pastor friends who lived nearby. I knew from watching my dad how busy most pastors are, and sure enough most of my dad's pastor friends made excuses and said they were too busy to come by. There was only one pastor, Sam Mayo, who came to visit my dad in the hospital. At the time, Sam Mayo was the pastor at the biggest church in the city and one of the fastest growing churches in the country. This church had 166 ministries that all reported to him. That's 166 meetings per week for Sam Mayo, and he had to also divide his time between preparing his messages and managing a multimillion-dollar budget.

When you're pastoring to thousands, I can only imagine how many of them end up in the hospital each week. If three people from my young adult group were in the hospital, I'd be overwhelmed, but Sam Mayo carved out time to go minister to someone who wasn't even a member of his church. He didn't gain anything from visiting my dad in the hospital. His offering didn't go up, the media wasn't there to report on it, and he didn't get any points from anyone but me. But he showed up anyway. The one person who had the most excuses not to show up and the least amount of free time is the one who did.

Eighteen years later when my dad had his second stroke, my parents were living in Atlanta. As soon as I heard the news I flew in from Dallas, wondering if this was it or if God would heal my dad again. I was the first of my brothers to show up at the hospital, and I spent an hour alone in the room with my dad. I stared at him lying peacefully in the hospital bed, thinking about what a full life he'd led and wondering if it was coming to an end. Over the course of that hour I prayed, I paced, and I spoke out loud. "I'm proud of you, Dad," I told him. "Can you hear me?"

Finally I went to sit down on the chair that was pulled up next to the bed and noticed a little prayer book that had been placed there. I opened up the twenty-page book, and inside was a business card with the name *Sam Mayo* on it. I let my head fall forward as I cried, amazed and touched by this man's faithfulness. Eighteen years later, Sam Mayo just happened to be working at another church in Atlanta. I don't even know how he heard about my dad, but he'd come that day, and he came back the next day, and the next day, and the day after that. Every day I was there, he came by and prayed with my family. After eighteen years and in another city, he was consistent, and it was awesome to see his character standing true.

Generosity doesn't have to cost money. Time is one of the most valuable assets in this world, and simply showing up for people is an incredibly generous thing to do. You may not have a lot of money, but we're all given twenty-four hours in a day. Make it your mission to use what you've been given to do something good. No matter what you have going on in your life, you can show up for people. Tell me if I'm wrong, but I think we all have one friend who's invited us to something recently. Maybe it's a birthday party, a benefit for a nonprofit, or even to hear the sales pitch for a pyramid scheme. That one friend would really love it if you'd show up, even if it's just to hear them out. I once gave my friend fifteen minutes to give me the whole sales pitch for his face lotion, and then I gave him my best business advice for how to improve his sales. He didn't get a sale from me, but I'd like to think I helped him get the next sale. We all get invited to things we don't want to go to, but sometimes just stopping by can go a long way.

Even when you're not invited, you can be on the lookout for ways to show up for people. Give a single mom you know a few hours off by taking her kids to the park. Go to that neighbor's house with the scary lawn and offer to mow it. This tells people that someone cares—not only that you care, but also that God cares. Whenever Amanda and I write a note of encouragement to someone, the first words we write are, "Hey, we just wanted you to know that God is thinking about you." People are often shocked to read this, but we tell them, "He put you in our hearts. God cares enough about you to put your name on the heart of two other individuals, and He imprinted it strong enough for us to act on it. We didn't pick your name out of a hat."

One of the very best habits you can create is being available for other people. Especially during hard times, simply showing up is the most meaningful thing you can do. During those dark hours, you don't need money and you don't need words; you just need someone sitting beside you. I pray that when it's all said and done, I'm not remembered for being on TV or even for writing a book. I hope people will remember that in my small corner of the world, I removed barriers so that I could be there for people.

To me, a selfish Christian is an oxymoron. If you say you're a Christian, you are telling me that you've been rescued from sin, that you've been forgiven for everything you've ever done wrong, and you've been given the same power and authority that raised Christ from the dead. You've been given so much, and Luke 12:48 tells us, "From everyone who has been given much, much will be demanded." When I stop to think about where I'd be without Jesus and all the passion, ideas, wisdom, and inspiration He has given me, it almost brings me to tears, and I give in a spirit of gratitude for everything I've been given. It just doesn't make sense to me that someone could receive all that and not respond generously.

Whenever I see an opportunity to help someone, I feel it's my duty to step in and act kindly as a representative of Christ. I'm constantly on the lookout for any possible way to give glory to Jesus. I wake up every morning with a fire in my belly, asking myself, "What can I do to be generous today?" This not only gives my entire life a purpose, but it also gives me a reason to give to others, to act generously to Amanda, and to share God's grace on earth.

It's clear to me that God has called Amanda and me to be generous. This is our purpose as a couple, and as you move toward joining with another person to become one, it's important to listen to God to find out what He has called you to do together. What is your mission as a couple? What is your marriage going to be about? The answers to these questions will set you on a path toward a marriage that's not only strong, lasting, and godly but also one that fulfills its destiny.

When you get married, you and your spouse will come together to become one, but that doesn't mean he or she will complete you. Marriage is not two half people coming together to form one whole; it's two complete people joining forces. And when you merge two people who are full of God's purpose for their lives, how can you not create an amazing love story out of that?

When two people come together who are activated and intentional about becoming the one, God can put you on an amazing mission. Maybe He'll send you to a third-world country to flip it upside down for His kingdom. Or maybe He'll have you start an organization for kids in your city. It might be as simple as volunteering for the youth ministry at your church, and that might not sound as exciting as someone else's destiny, but there is greatness in anything that God calls you to do. The kids who see you at church may never get a front-row seat to another marriage, and what they see in you two may change their whole perspective.

An amazing love story starts with you, but you're not meant to be together just for you. When God brings the best "you" together with the best Mr. or Miss Right, it's so you can be the picture of His love in the world. Wherever you go—near or far—you'll shine a light for everyone around you. Your amazing love story and the kindness you show will make an impact that can change the world. When Amanda and I saw that we had over a million views on our documentary, we weren't excited about the notoriety; we were grateful for the opportunity to make an impact.

You may never do anything that goes viral, and maybe you'll never start an organization that drastically shifts the culture of a third-world country, but you still have the opportunity to make an impact by shifting culture for a widow, orphan, single mom, or teen in the youth group of your local church. Sometimes being the one starts with changing one's life and doing for your spouse what you wish you could do for everyone. What might this look like for you? Can you imagine creating a home where your kids think of Christmas completely different from their friends and wake up on Christmas morning excited to go to the homeless shelter? Can you picture giving one child at church a front-row seat to a godly marriage and then watching that child go off and change the world? Imagine who God has called you to be and what life will look like when you become the one, then envision your marriage as a way of doubling your impact so you can shine your light twice as brightly wherever it's needed most.

One Question to Ask Yourself: Ten years from now, what do you want your family to be known for?

One Thing to Remember: An amazing love story starts with you.

One Thing to Work On: Write out a vision statement for your future family.

Afterword

I am sending you out like sheep among wolves. Therefore be as shrewd as snakes and as innocent as doves.
Be on your guard; you will be handed over to the local
councils and be flogged in the synagogues. On my
account you will be brought before governors and kings
as witnesses to them and to the Gentiles. But when they
arrest you, do not worry about what to say or how to
say it. At that time you will be given what to say, for it
will not be you speaking, but the Spirit of your Father
speaking through you.

—Matthew 10:16–20

I f you pay close attention to the first nine chapters in the gospel of Matthew, you'll notice that Jesus's disciples kind of followed Him blindly
without any instructions. Matthew 10 is the first time in Scripture that
we see Jesus give specific directions. This is Jesus's first staff meeting,
and He sits down with His disciples and tells them how things are
going to be, how they're going to operate, and what's going to happen
to them if they're on His team. It starts on a high note as He tells them
to travel from town to town and "drive out impure spirits and to heal

every disease and sickness" (v. 1). If you read this passage slowly, you can almost feel the excitement in the room as the disciples learn about what life is going to be like with Jesus on their side. They're going to heal the sick and raise the dead! (See v. 8.) Then things suddenly start to go downhill. "You will be handed over to the local councils and be flogged in the synagogues," Jesus tells them. "You will be hated by everyone because of me" (vv. 17, 22).

What Jesus was asking His disciples to do wasn't easy. It took strength, bravery, and most of all, faith to go out "like a sheep among wolves" (v. 16). We know what we're asking you to do isn't easy either. You can easily read this book and feel the weight of a whole list of things you need to do. We get that. And we know it's much easier to settle for the guy or girl who happens to be sitting next to you in class or at church than it is to wait patiently for God to bring the right one into your life. It's more romantic to fall in love with someone who has the right car, looks, or job than it is to intentionally create a godly love within the covenant of marriage. It's sexier to flirt with temptation than it is to flee from sexual immorality. Perhaps most of all, it's easier to focus on what you're looking for in a mate and all the ways someone fails to live up to your standards than it is to raise your standard for yourself and devote this season of your life to becoming the one you were meant to be.

But just like Jesus's disciples, you don't have to face these challenges alone. As His disciples started to absorb the gravity of what they had to do, Jesus spoke words of encouragement, and what He said to them then can sustain you through anything you face in life, certainly including this. He knew how much He was asking of them, and He said,

"What I tell you in the dark, speak in the daylight; what is whispered in your ear, proclaim from the roofs" (v. 27).

This is the quote we go back to when the chips are down. Back when we were questioning whether or not to move forward with our relationship, later when we had ten dollars in our bank account, and more recently when we've watched some of our family members fall ill, we felt helpless and confused. But we knew that all we could do was listen for the whisper. And whenever we've taken a pause and really listened, there's always been a little whisper there. It's enough to keep us going, and it's that same whisper that gets us up in the morning, motivates us to act with intention in our marriage, inspires us to give freely to others, and gives us the strength to fight against sin and selfishness.

You've just read an entire book filled with our advice, and we pray that you've learned something that will help you embrace this season of your life as you prepare for the next one. But the very best advice we could ever give you is to keep on listening for that whisper and proclaiming what you hear from the roofs. It's what you hear in those quiet moments that will give you the strength to keep going, keep striving, and keep reaching further until you become the one God has called you to be.

Acknowledgments

I t would truly take another book to acknowledge every person who's helped us along our journey and specifically, those who made this book happen.

Jesus, thank you. For your life and for writing our story from the beginning. Never let us go.

Family, thank you. For raising us. For praying for us. For your joy and laughter. You make it hard to be in a bad mood.

Friends, thank you. For listening. For all the airport rides. For rebounding. For helping raise Jaxson. We are strong because you are strong.

Our church, thank you. For your generosity and wisdom. There's no place like home.

Foundry Media Group, thank you. For taking a chance on a young couple and representing us with excellence.

The WaterBrook publishing team, thank you. For believing in us. Our amazing love story continues on because of you.

Jodi Lipper, thank you. For putting your girls in day care so that authors like us can succeed. For helping our voices make sense on paper.